In this book Lisa Derhake seeks to show us how the truth of the words of the Good Shepherd, 'I know my own and my own know me' can really impact our lives and bring fulfilment in a way that being known (or not) by anyone else can never truly satisfy. Written from personal experience of the depths of despair this book shows how being soaked in the Word of God can be a powerful tool to pull us out of the pits of life.

It stirs my heart to hear the words of the good shepherd call out to me that I am known, this book can help us gaze afresh on the wonder it is that the God of the Universe knows us more intimately than anyone else and what satisfaction and fulfilment that brings.

Anna Putt
Keswick Ministries trustee
Host of Shielded by Grace Podcast

Writing from the depth of her biblical knowledge and life experiences, Lisa Derhake guides readers through a 10-week Bible study of Psalm 23. I expect many people to walk closer to the Great Shepherd as a result of this fine book.

Robert L. Plummer
Collin and Evelyn Aikman Professor of Biblical Studies, The Southern Baptist Theological Seminary, Louisville, Kentucky
Author of several books, including *40 Questions About Interpreting the Bible*

Through a carefully prepared study, employing thoughtful and insightful questions, Lisa guides us to discover for ourselves the beauty of our great shepherd and the impactful privilege of being known by Him. Beginning in Psalm 23, she takes us on a journey through various passages of Scripture which illuminate and illustrate in God's own words, what it means to be shepherded by Him. Lisa's own experience with these passages, her faithfulness to the inspired

Word, and her commitment to transformative application make this study one that is sure to encourage, change, and stir in all of us a deeper love for the Good Shepherd!

Nora Allison
Formerly Director of Women's Ministry at Sojourn East, Louisville, Kentucky

Lisa's devotional book is helpful for all but especially poignant for anyone who battles discouragement and depression. It's helpful not only because Lisa has been 'relentlessly sucked into the black hole of depression' herself but because of the many meaningful Scripture references and the daily assignments that point to the way out.

Bob Russell
Secretary, Evangelical Theological Society
Author of several books, including *Embodied: Living as Whole People in a Fractured World*

I'm thankful for this timely yet timeless study of a classic scripture. Lisa skillfully guides us into the pattern, promise and practice of Psalm 23. This is a much needed word for our anxious souls in these anxious times. I was stirred to simultaneously dig deep and simply delight in this wonderful Psalm.

Daniel Montgomery
Founder and CEO of Leadership Reality, author of *Proof, Leadership Mosaic,* and *How to Be Present in an Absent World*

Lisa Derhake is not a household name; in fact, this is the first book she's written. And I highly recommend it! As one of her pastors, I've witnessed the deep and expansive study in which she engages as she interprets biblical texts. I've seen the extensive effort in wordsmithing that she puts forth as she seeks to communicate biblical truth with clarity and precision. I've experienced the practical application of her teaching as women's lives are changed by her biblical instruction and exhortation. You don't know Lisa Derhake, but I attest to her excellent work. More importantly, you will be Known by our Good Shepherd as you follow her ten-week study of Psalm 23.

Gregg R. Allison

Professor of Christian Theology, The Southern Baptist Theological Seminary, Louisville, Kentucky

Author of several books including *Embodied: Living as Whole People in a Fractured World*

To feel loved, we must be known. This devotional guides us into an astonishing, mind-blowing awareness of what happens when we realize that God knows every fiber and fold of who we are and He treasures us.

Jesse Eubanks

Founder and Executive Director of Love Thy Neighborhood & co-host of Love Thy Neighborhood podcast

Author of *How We Relate*

KNOWN

A Study of the
Good Shepherd

Lisa Derhake

CHRISTIAN
FOCUS

Hardback ISBN   978-1-5271-0838-7
Ebook ISBN   978-1-5271-0907-0

10 9 8 7 6 5 4 3 2 1

Published in 2022
by
Christian Focus Publications Ltd,
Geanies House, Fearn, Ross-shire,
IV20 1TW, Scotland, Great Britain

www.christianfocus.com

Designed by Daniel Van Straaten

Printed by Gutenberg, Malta

CONTENTS

INTRODUCTION

Who am I? Does anyone really know me? It is human nature to long to be known. In our culture today we see this longing on display everywhere we turn. We want others to see us. We want to matter in this world. We long for recognition and fame. Reality television capitalizes on our longing to be known. Shows run the gamut from searching for love, like on *The Bachelor,* to trying new endeavors, like primal living on *Naked and Afraid,* to ballroom dancing on *Dancing with the Stars.* One glance at Instagram or Facebook and we instantly encounter this longing to be seen, to be heard and to be known in every post. These avenues give us ways to be known— to an extent—but don't we long for something more? Beneath it all, under the clever posts about the latest antics of a crazy dog or educated musings on the anti-vax movement or your kiddo's unintentionally funny comment, we all have a deep, unwavering longing to be known.

The unquenchable search for fame or recognition or an engaging response to an online post might provide momentary relief from our need to be known, but the relief is fleeting. We can be known partially and temporarily in this world, but we will never feel fully known by others, even when those people are our spouses or our best friends. We might tend to get disheartened when we think of the limitations of being known to others in this world, but I would like

9

us to flip our frustrations. What if we consider—for just a moment—that it might be a beautiful thing that other people *cannot* fulfill this longing? What if we change the internal narrative that runs through our minds?

I think that God allows us to be acutely aware of the unfulfilled longing to be known so that we draw closer to Him. If my husband Brian knows me so fully and completely that he can anticipate and provide for my every need and desire and he never misunderstands a word that I say (wouldn't *that* be a life-changer?!), what need would I have of the Lord? This question can be asked of any person with whom you have a close relationship—a friend, a mother, a father, a daughter, a son, a sister, a brother. If anyone on this earth can completely fulfill our desires to be known, where does the Lord fit? We search for ways to be known in this world. We chase dreams in the hope of leaving our mark. We pour boundless energy into blogs in the hopes that our site might go viral. We audition for the next show, we study for the mother of all tests, we train for marathons, we write speeches and we build innovative businesses. We sit in coffee shops writing books so that we feel purpose and others might know that purpose. (Guilty as charged.) But—but, what if all we really need is to truly understand that we are *already* fully and completely and beautifully known?

Now I'm not proposing that our efforts to be known are all bad. Dreams are beautiful, and they can drive us to accomplish great works that God has given us to do. Books published, art displayed, promotions earned, classes taught, performances nailed, races run, research funded—these are all amazing outcomes of hard work and dedication to dreams, to becoming known just a little bit more in this finite world of ours. However, when we disproportionately place our hopes and desires of being fulfilled and being known through avenues such as these, we cripple ourselves from becoming all that God has given us to be in Him. Until we can really grasp that we are His and He knows us fully, we will feel like something is missing. In John 10:14 Jesus says, 'I know my own and my own know me.'

This book was borne out of my own search to be known. I didn't even realize how intently I was focused on fulfilling this need until my life seemed to crash down around me. A perfect storm of events landed me in a deep pit of clinical depression. Never before had I ever felt so low and never before had I fully understood the nature of the disease. I did not think that depression was something that *this* girl typing *these* words would ever or could ever experience. How wrong I was, and how humbled I became. Praise God! I mean that sincerely. Through this trial, God has grown me in ways I never could have foreseen.

When I felt that I had absolutely nothing, He showed me that I have everything. When I was broken beyond repair, He was at work refining my soul. Proverbs 25:4 says, 'Take away the dross from the silver, and the smith has material for the vessel.' The Lord is the great silversmith who was in the process of removing impurities (the dross) from His daughter's soul. My refining was part of the Holy Spirit graciously conforming me more into the image of the Son. When I felt completely broken, like I had absolutely nothing to offer this world, God the Father, Son and Holy Spirit were all mysteriously at work in me, cleaning me up and reshaping me to be the vessel they desire me to be. This did not happen overnight; in fact, the reshaping and polishing is ongoing and will continue until I am home with the Lord. There is great pain in the process, but there is also undeniable beauty in the refining.

The Lord comforted me through Psalm 23. *The Lord is my shepherd; I shall not want.* One of the most well-known psalms. I read it,

11

prayed it and meditated on it from a very new perspective—one of desperation. I recited it during sleepless nights when my body felt electrified by anxiety and physiologically could not relax. I pleaded and I groaned. Oftentimes I felt like He was gone, like He wasn't listening, that somehow He didn't know that I could not endure another moment of the agony—but in my head I knew this was false. I found it nearly impossible to convince my heart otherwise, but I kept praying and seeking. As time went on at an excruciatingly sluggish pace, I slowly began to feel His presence. Among other modalities, part of my healing came through extensive meditation and study of Psalm 23. I came to know the Lord as *my* shepherd in a precious new way that could not have been attained without the trial by fire. In the process, He assured me that I am fully and completely known.

My prayer in writing this book is that you too will find great comfort from your Shepherd. Don't rush it—the process takes time. It's worth it, though. By seeking the Lord in Scripture, you will find Him and you will grow closer to Him, and in doing so you will also discover (or *re*discover) the beautiful truth that in Him you are known and you truly have all that you need. As our Shepherd, God personally loves and cares for each of His sheep as individual, unique creations. We will see in Psalm 23 and throughout Scripture that the Lord cares for us completely, gives us rest, restores our souls, leads us in righteousness, is with us in our suffering, provides comfort, prepares a place for us, provides abundantly and gives us eternal hope. Because He does all this and more, as believers we can find comfort in Him, whether we are experiencing life from a glorious mountaintop or traversing the darkest valley. In a world where we often ask, *'Does anyone really know me? Do I even matter?'* the truth stands: YOU ARE KNOWN.

CHAPTER 1

THE GOOD SHEPHERD
Studying a theme in the Bible

It was during one of the sleepless nights when my shoulders and back were lit up with electrodes of anxiety that I heard God speak to me. It was not an audible voice, but rather a still, small sense that I felt emanating from the core of my body. As a believer I *know* that the Holy Spirit mysteriously dwells within me, but this was one of those rare moments where I could tangibly *feel* His presence. As I was reciting Psalm 23 silently in the dark, I suddenly just knew that I was meant to study this psalm in depth, and not to just study it but also to share it and specifically to write a Bible study on it. I had a little conversation with God—*but how, Lord? You know I want to write, but this is so different from anything I've envisioned. I thought my days for writing were still many years down the road—once the kids are out of the house and my time frees up a bit! I thought I would write studies that focused on working straight through one book of the Bible at a time. God, this is so different. How do I do this?* The answer I heard was not a complete answer, but it was a sense that I was supposed to trust Him and move forward in devotional times, digging deeply into the psalm, cross-referencing other sections of Scripture, and focusing on allowing my mind to heal. He told me (again, not in explicit words!)

that this is a project that will take time. Do. Not. Rush. It. The biggest thing I walked away with from that conversation was that He just wanted me to meet with Him; the rest would come in His time. Little did I know how deeply I would be blessed in the years to come by the countless hours spent with Him on this project.

The first time I settled down in the old, sage green plush glider that harkened back from my days with babies but now graced the corner of our master suite instead of the nursery, I really did not know how to begin the journey, but God did! As I quietly sat, journal in hand, I felt led to do a search on my Bible app[1] to find references to sheep and shepherding throughout the Bible, beginning in Genesis and ending in Revelation. It was an amazing exercise. Not one for the faint of heart, I assure you, as this cross-referencing took a serious chunk of time, but if you have never experienced depression I have to let you in on a little secret here. Anything to combat the endless hours of desperation is a welcome reprieve to the despair and negative self-talk that normally fills the brain during this distorted, *ab*normal state of mind. And you know what God did with that little exercise? He used it as the framework for all the time I would spend with Him in the months and years to come. He gave me a plan!

All that to say, before we move forward with our scriptural study of God as a shepherd, I encourage you to take the time to sit with this theme and actually trace it through the Bible for yourself. Spend anywhere from five minutes to several hours or days or weeks discovering what the Lord has for you as you look up different references to sheep and shepherds. For those who are strapped for time, I have included my own work in the appendix! As a disclaimer, my outline is not a *complete* cross-referencing work, so please don't

---

1   YouVersion Bible app.

hold me to that standard! I have really provided it as an example and as a tool for you to use in your own personal study.

Several months after beginning this process, I attended an amazing, albeit intense, conference led by Bible teacher Nancy Guthrie. Wouldn't you know, I discovered that I had been doing something along the lines of what Nancy taught as biblical theology—tracing a theme of the Bible throughout the entirety of Scripture. Studying Scripture in this way can help us to see the Lord in an entirely new light and to see His character and purposes from the beginning of time all the way into the future. The cross-referencing that I have done in the back is loosely based on Nancy's method that she taught at the conference. You will see how I chronologically worked through the Bible in categories[2], finding references to sheep, shepherds, and shepherding as I tackled each section:

- Creation
- The Fall
- Pentateuch (Genesis–Deuteronomy)
- Old Testament History (Judges–Esther)
- Old Testament Wisdom (Job–Song of Songs)
- Old Testament Prophets (Isaiah–Malachi)
- The Gospels, Cross/Resurrection/Ascension/ Pentecost (Gospels and Acts)
- Epistles (Letters of the New Testament)
- Consummation (Revelation and other New Testament references to the future)

You can do this too! I promise. It is not as daunting as it sounds, and in this rapidly progressive age of technology that we currently inhabit,

---

2 'Biblical Theology Workshop for Women with Nancy Guthrie' at Sojourn Church East, September 20-21, 2019.

there are boundless resources literally at our fingertips. I personally love the YouVersion app for its accessibility and convenience but I also love my three-inch thick hardback biblical concordance[3]. Whatever resource you find easiest, use it! Type words like 'sheep,' 'shepherd,' and 'shepherding' in the search bar or flip through your book until you find them, and then start at the beginning. See what you can find in Genesis and move forward book by book, jotting down references to the scripture verses that you discover. If any (or all!) of them jump out at you or have special significance in your life, take a few notes next to the reference so that you can easily go back to them at any time. I promise you, friends, it is worth your time to study the Scriptures in this way, and it will give you the best overview you can have before we jump full-force into this study.

HOMEWORK & REFLECTION

For each section of the Bible, write down at least one cross-referenced verse that has meaning to you and explain why. I have broken this down into days so that you do not feel overwhelmed by the prospect of doing it all at once.

DAY 1

- Creation

....

....

....

....

---

3   *The Strongest NIV Exhaustive Concordance.*

....

....

- The Fall

....

....

....

....

....

....

DAY 2

- Pentateuch (Genesis–Deuteronomy)

....

....

....

....

....

....

- Old Testament History (Judges–Esther)

....

....

....

....

....

....

DAY 3

- Old Testament Wisdom (Job–Song of Songs)

....

....

....

....

....

....

- Old Testament Prophets (Isaiah–Malachi)

....

....

....

....

....

....

DAY 4

- The Gospels, Cross/Resurrection/Ascension/Pentecost
  (Gospels and Acts)

....

....

....

....

....

....

• Epistles (Letters of the New Testament)

....

....

....

....

....

....

• Consummation (Revelation and other New Testament
  references to the future)

....

....

....

....

....

....

DAY 5

1. What is one new thing you learned about the Lord by tracing the
    theme of sheep/shepherd/shepherding throughout the Bible?

    ....

    ....

    ....

    ....

    ....

    ....

2. Evaluate the current season of life in which you find yourself—
    are you feeling dry and parched, well-watered and fruitful, or
    somewhere in-between?

    ....

    ....

    ....

    ....

    ....

    ....

3. What does it mean to you personally when you hear the
    statement, 'The Lord is my shepherd'?

    ....

    ....

    ....

    ....

    ....

    ....

CHAPTER 2

THE LORD IS MY SHEPHERD

PSALM 23

The LORD is my shepherd; I shall not want.
He makes me lie down in green pastures.
He leads me beside still waters.
He restores my soul.
He leads me in paths of righteousness
for his name's sake.

Even though I walk through the valley of the shadow of death,
I will fear no evil,
for you are with me;
your rod and your staff,
they comfort me.

You prepare a table before me
in the presence of my enemies;
you anoint my head with oil;
my cup overflows.
Surely goodness and mercy shall follow me
all the days of my life,
and I shall dwell in the house of the LORD forever.

This week we will be studying Psalm 23 in depth, and in subsequent weeks we will study other passages throughout Scripture that speak truth about our life with the Shepherd as encountered in Psalm 23. Psalm 23 is an individual psalm of trust. Other individual psalms of trust include 4, 16, 27, 62 and 73. There are also community psalms of trust, which include Psalms 90, 115, 123, 124, 125 and 126.[1]

The first goal for you this week is to memorize Psalm 23. Practice a little every day, adding on one verse at a time, and before you know it, you will have these six sweet verses memorized and easily accessible in times of need and in times of plenty. Let me be the first to tell you that memorizing Scripture is not some sort of magic pill to ease your woes, but it is an excellent discipline to establish so that you can hold onto God's Word in your heart and draw near to Him.

After having one of those emotionally charged nights when I found sleep to be elusive, I wrote this in my journal in the wee hours of the morning: *My Good Shepherd brought peace as I finally conceded to losing sleep after waking up at 2:45 a.m. I* will *survive sleepless nights and nights with little rest. He is my rest. He makes me lie down in green pastures. He leads me beside quiet waters. He restores my soul. I will fear no evil for YOU are with me.* These were achingly desperate words whispered in the dead of night during a moment when I felt stripped to the core. I had absolutely *nothing,* not even the reprieve of sleep, but I had Him. And He is exactly what each and every one of us needs.

HOMEWORK & REFLECTION

DAY 1

1. First take some time to pray to God about the time you are going to spend with Him. Now read slowly through Psalm 23. Meditate

---

1 Bullock, C. Hassell. *Teach the Text Commentary Series: Psalms, Vol. 1: Psalms 1–72.*

on each phrase, word and idea. Read it several times through, perhaps even out loud or in a different Bible version.[2] Use the cross-references in the footnotes of your Bible if you like. Jot down anything that comes to mind as God's Word speaks to you. This practice will really help you own it.

....

....

....

....

....

....

2. Notice any repeated words and phrases and any patterns you see in Psalm 23. Take note of the pronouns (i.e. I, you, he, me, etc.) and where they occur. Discuss the tone of the psalm.

....

....

....

....

....

....

DAY 2

1. In verses 1-4, we encounter the first metaphor of Psalm 23 in which the psalmist compares himself to a sheep and the Lord to

2 I have grown to love the ESV (English Standard Version) in recent years but like to study from my 1984 NIV (New International Version) as well. The YouVersion app also gives me access to many other great options.

a Shepherd. Let's focus our attention today on verses 1-3. Look at the verbs in these three verses and write them down.

....

....

....

....

....

....

2. Do you notice anything in particular when you examine the verbs? Observe *who* the Lord *is,* look at what this means to the psalmist about his own personal state of being, and look at what the Lord *does.* Write down your thoughts about what the psalmist is declaring here.

....

....

....

....

....

....

3. What do you think the psalmist means when he uses the phrases 'green pastures' and 'still waters'? What do these phrases mean to you personally? What do green pastures and still waters look like in your life?

....

....

....

....

....

....

4. Have you ever experienced the Lord restoring your soul? Explain
    what happened.

....

....

....

....

....

....

5. What do you think it means to be led in paths of righteousness? Why
    does God lead us in paths of righteousness, according to verse 3?

....

....

....

....

....

....

DAY 3

1. Today we are going to study verse 4 in depth. We are still in the
    section of the psalm that falls under the metaphor of a shepherd

and sheep, but we see another metaphor embedded within this one: the valley of the shadow of death. What is the psalmist referring to when he uses this illustration?

....

....

....

....

....

....

2. What two words (verb and preposition) does the psalmist use in describing his encounter with the valley? (Hint: they come immediately *before* the phrase 'the valley of the shadow of death.') Why are these words significant?

....

....

....

....

....

....

3. The psalmist makes a strong declaration, 'I will fear no evil.' Why does he not fear? (Notice the change in pronouns used for the Lord here. In verses 1-3 we see the psalmist using 'he' and 'his.' Now in verse 4 the song becomes very personal as he transitions to using the pronoun 'you.')

....

....

....

....

....

....

4. Do the words 'I will fear no evil' resonate with you? Why or why not? What evil do you fear? What would it look like for you to trust the Lord with these fears?

....

....

....

....

....

....

DAY 4

Let's look at the final two verses of Psalm 23 today. While verses 1–4 use the metaphor of the divine Shepherd and a sheep, in verses 5 and 6 the metaphor is altered a bit. We still encounter the divine Shepherd, but now instead of a sheep, we see allusions to a king.

1. Read Isaiah 25. After meditating over this chapter in Isaiah, what are your thoughts about the table in Psalm 23:5?

....

....

....

....

....

....

....

2. In verse 5, what makes us think of a king? (Hint: read 1 Samuel 16:13)

....

....

....

....

....

....

3. Read verse 6 in several Bible translations. What differences do you find? Does a particular translation resonate more strongly with you and, if so, why?

....

....

....

....

....

....

4. What is *following* the psalmist? Now read Psalm 43:3-4 and write down what it is that the psalmist desires to *lead* him. Psalm 43 is part of the song of lament found within Psalms 42-43. (Scholars think these two psalms go together as one.) Look at what the psalmist longs for and rejoices in as he closes his song of lament. Now go back to Psalm 23 and discuss the joy found in verse 6.

....

....

....

....

....

....

DAY 5

Spend some time today digesting what you have unearthed over the past several days as you have faithfully studied Psalm 23. Read it over again, reciting it out loud if you can. Polish it in your memory.

1. Is there a particular part of this psalm that really stuck out to you? Why?

....

....

....

....

....

....

2. Has your study of Psalm 23 deepened your understanding of the character of God? Please explain.

....

....

....

....

....

....

3. Is there hope for you to be found in this psalm? After having done the soul-stretching work of studying Psalm 23 verse-by-verse and learning more about God through it, think about how it applies to your life. Surely, we can all agree that the psalmist felt *known* by the Lord. As you read Psalm 23, are you able to see how you are known by God as well?

    Be honest here. If your answer is 'yes,' praise the Lord and share that. If your answer is more along the lines of 'no' or 'maybe sometimes,' hang in there! Keep on working through this study because God's Word does not return empty. When you seek Him you will find Him.

....

....

....

....

....

....

As Matthew Henry, a nonconformist minister of the late seventeenth and early eighteenth centuries, wrote about Jesus' *Ask, Seek, Knock*[3] discourse of Matthew 7:7, '*Seek*, as for a thing of value that we have lost, or as the merchantman that *seeks goodly pearls. Seek by prayer*… Seeking and knocking imply something more than asking and praying. We must not only *ask* but *seek*; we must second our prayers with our endeavors; we must, in the use of the appointed means, *seek* for that which we *ask* for…God gives knowledge and grace to those that

---

3 https://www.biblegateway.com/resources/matthew-henry/Matt.7.7-Matt.7.11 Last accessed November 2021.

search the Scriptures, and wait at Wisdom's gates; and power against sin to those that avoid the occasions of it…we must *seek* diligently; we must continue knocking; must persevere in prayer, and in the use of means; must endure to the end in the duty' (*Matthew Henry's Commentary*).

Please share your struggles so that others can pray for you, love you, and spur you on in your faith. God has given us one another to bear each other's burdens. Allow the beautiful body of Christ to step in and be the support that you need in this season.

CHAPTER 3

JESUS the SHEPHERD
John 10

The LORD is my shepherd; I shall not want.
PSALM 23:1

Toward the beginning of my arduous journey out of the pit, one of the first places in the Bible to which the Holy Spirit led me was John chapter 10. It stirred so many emotions within me, emotions that needed to be awakened because my soul had been relentlessly sucked into the black hole of depression. I felt like a walking shell of a person.

I read 'The sheep hear his voice' (v. 3), and my heart broke with longing to hear *only* His voice rather than the whispers of the enemy as that wretched creature spun lies in my head.

'A stranger they will not follow, but they will flee from him…' (v. 5). How I longed to flee from this sinister stranger but for some strange, supernatural reason I could not escape him. He has a measure of authority in this world, and I need the Lord at all times to arm me against his evil schemes.

'I am the door. If anyone enters by me, he will be saved and will go in and out and find pasture' (v. 9). I praised the Lord, resting secure in the knowledge of my salvation, and finding that my only true rest during this disease came when I was able to find pasture in Him.

'I came that they may have life and have it abundantly' (v. 10). One day I wrote in my journal, *Jesus came so that I might flourish—live life*

to the full. Abundantly. It is for freedom that I have been set free (Gal. 5:1).
For the whole law is fulfilled in one word: you shall love your neighbor
as yourself (Gal. 5:14). I have been set free to <u>love</u>; to love <u>well</u>. Dear Lord,
help me to love well in my mothering, as a wife, as a daughter and as a
friend. Praise be to God! In my weakness you are strong. Let me rely on your
strength every day, every moment. I love you. Amen. Isaiah 53:6 says 'We
all, like sheep, have gone astray…' (NIV). I am that sheep who has gone
astray, but our God is in the business of rescuing His children, and He
rescued me with an unabashed love that knows no end.

'I am the good shepherd. The good shepherd lays down his life
for the sheep' (v. 11). As I thought of this extravagant sacrifice that my
Shepherd King made for me and for every single one of His precious
children, I wept—greater love has no one than this.

'I am the good shepherd. I know my own and my own know
me' (v. 14). *I AM KNOWN.* What a reason to rejoice! Without a doubt,
no matter how lonely I feel, my Shepherd knows me. These words
began to fill the cracks and crevices of my broken soul. They were
like the liquid bandage that held me together as the healing
began. They gave me strength that I had not felt in months. Most
of all, they sparked a determination that I would fight this disease
with everything in me because the Creator of the universe was
the one providing my armor and weaponry. I was reminded of
Ephesians 6:14-18:

> Stand therefore, having fastened on the belt of truth, and having
> put on the breastplate of righteousness, and, as shoes for your
> feet, having put on the readiness given by the gospel of peace. In
> all circumstances take up the shield of faith, with which you can
> extinguish all the flaming darts of the evil one; and take the helmet
> of salvation, and the sword of the Spirit, which is the word of God,
> praying at all times in the Spirit, with all prayer and supplication.

I was not left alone to fight the battle. God was before me and behind me, surrounding me completely with His perfect love and reminding me that I am one of His own and He knows me. And not only does He know me like this, but He knows *every single one* of His children like this.

'So there will be one flock, one shepherd' (v. 16). He will demolish all the barriers that divide us in this world—the broken will be made whole. Our hope will be fully realized when Revelation 7:9-12 comes to pass.

> After this I looked, and behold, a great multitude that no one could number, from every nation, from all tribes and peoples and languages, standing before the throne and before the Lamb, clothed in white robes, with palm branches in their hands, and crying out with a loud voice, 'Salvation belongs to our God who sits on the throne, and to the Lamb!' And all the angels were standing around the throne and around the elders and the four living creatures, and they fell on their faces before the throne and worshiped God, saying, 'Amen! Blessing and glory and wisdom and thanksgiving and honor and power and might be to our God forever and ever! Amen.'

John 10 is so rich with substance and sustenance. It will nourish our souls as we learn more about our great Savior, the Lamb who was slain, the Shepherd of our souls. 'I know my own and my own know me.' He knows you. He knows what makes your heart break, what causes your emotions to soar, what overwhelms you with joy, what drags you to the depths of despair. He knows your every thought, your every breath, your every longing and desire. Not only does He *know* you, but He *loves* you with a love far deeper than anything you can possibly imagine. The proof is in His death. The life is in His resurrection. Praise be to God.

HOMEWORK & REFLECTION

DAY 1

1. Read slowly through John 10. Meditate on each phrase, word and idea. Read it several times through, perhaps even out loud. Use the cross-references in the footnotes of your Bible if you like. Jot down anything that comes to mind as God's Word speaks to you. This practice will really help you own it.

....

....

....

....

....

....

2. Notice any repeated words or phrases. Write down what you think their significance might be. Find all references to sheep and shepherds and any other imagery used in this passage. Record your thoughts as God's Word speaks to you.

....

....

....

....

....

....

DAY 2

1. Let's focus on verses 1-6 today. Before anything else though, go back and read the story recorded in John 9 so that you better

understand the context of Jesus' discourse in chapter 10. In John 9 we see Jesus perform a mind-blowing miracle! He heals a man born blind, and that man exclaims, 'Never since the world began has it been heard that anyone opened the eyes of a man born blind. If this man were not from God, he could do nothing' (9:32-33). The unbelieving Pharisees are infuriated and Jesus is compassionate. We see a beautiful eyewitness account of a man coming to faith in this chapter. And we also see Jesus pointedly calling out the Pharisees. Record any observations you have of John 9 that really speak to you.

....

....

....

....

....

....

2. Now read through John 10:1-6 and let your mind ponder these verses. How do these words of Jesus that immediately follow His pronouncement to the Pharisees, 'If you were blind, you would have no guilt; but now that you say, "We see," your guilt remains' (9:41), relate to that pronouncement? What thread do you see joining John 9 and John 10?

....

....

....

....

....

....

3. When you read verses 1-6, what makes sense? What puzzles you? After answering these questions, spend some time praying to God for wisdom and understanding as you continue studying His Word. Thank Him for revealing Himself to you and don't be afraid to ask Him for more! Praise Him for being the great God that He is.

....

....

....

....

....

....

DAY 3

1. Our focus today will be on verses 7-21, but we're first going to look back in Scripture, this time not just one chapter back but several centuries. Read Ezekiel 34:1-10 and then read John 10:7-21. How does the Ezekiel passage expand your understanding of what Jesus is saying to the Pharisees here?

....

....

....

....

....

....

2. What do you think Jesus means when he says, 'I am the door of the sheep' (v. 7)?

....

....

....

....

....

....

3. In your life, what does it look like to have life 'abundantly'
   (John 10:10)? Do you experience the abundant life? Do you
   struggle to grasp the meaning of this abundance?

....

....

....

....

....

....

4. Contrast the good shepherd with the thief/robber in verses 1, 5,
   8, and 10 and the hired hand in verses 12-13.

....

....

....

....

....

....

5. Look at how many times Jesus talks about laying down His life in this passage. Read those verses and then focus in on verses 17-18. Discuss Jesus' authority. What is Jesus' role in His own death? Where does He get His authority?

....

....

....

....

....

....

6. We would be remiss to skip over the reaction of the Jews to these unprecedented words from the lips of Jesus. What do you see happening in verses 19-21?

....

....

....

....

....

....

DAY 4

1. Read through John 10:22-39. About two months have passed between verse 21 and verse 22. The Feast of Dedication is what we know of as Hanukkah, which is a Hebrew word that means 'dedication.' It celebrates the result of the Maccabean Revolt from 167–160 B.C. in which Judas Maccabaeus led the Jewish people against a madman named Antiochus Epiphanes, who began ruling in the area in 175 B.C. and completely desecrated the Temple.

Ultimately the revolutionaries cleansed the Temple and reinstated proper Jewish worship there, and the Feast of Dedication was instituted to remember and celebrate this victory.[1]

So here we have Jesus, walking in the Temple during this Feast, and the Jews (these are the unbelieving Jews) confront Jesus. What do they say to Him and how does He respond?

....

....

....

....

....

....

2. What warning do you find implied in Jesus' words in verses 25-29? What security does Jesus offer?

....

....

....

....

....

....

3. Do you experience this security in your day-to-day life? Explain.

....

....

1   Hughes, R. Kent. *John: That You May Believe*, pp. 275-6.

....

....

....

....

4. The tension is at an extremely high point in verse 31. The unbelieving Jews are ready to put Jesus to death—why? What do you think of Jesus' response to them in verses 32-38?

....

....

....

....

....

....

5. Read Psalm 82:6. Does this help you understand John 10:34-36 at all? Jesus is basically saying, 'If you want to get technical, it is not blasphemy for me to call myself the Son of God.' In the same breath, however, He asserts that He most definitely is God. Comment on John 10:37-38.

....

....

....

....

....

....

DAY 5

1. Now read John 10:39-42. Just picture this emotionally charged scene, where voices surely were not gentle. Imagine the riotous nature of it all, the men ready to stone Jesus, on the verge of violence, shouting at Him, jeering at His words. They try to arrest Him and lead Him to His death. Jesus is close to the road to Calvary but isn't there just yet. His hour has not yet come, and He evades the Jews who are trying to destroy Him. His work on the earth is not finished. What beautiful scene do you encounter in verses 40-41 that is in stark contrast to the scene from which Jesus just escaped?

....

....

....

....

....

....

2. Read John 1:19-34. What did John the Baptist testify about Jesus?

....

....

....

....

....

....

3. What was John the Baptist's purpose as we read in John 1:6-8?

....

....

....

....

....

....

4. What is the result of Jesus' actions in this place (see v. 42)?

....

....

....

....

....

....

5. Now read John 20:30-31. These verses actually sum up the pur-
    pose that John the Evangelist had when he wrote this Gospel.
    Write down what you find in 20:31.

....

....

....

....

....

....

The word 'life' in verse 31 is not just eternal life, but it also refers to
the life here and now that is experienced as a believer in Christ. It is

the abundant life that Jesus promised in John 10:10. We don't have to wait for heaven to have life in His name! Take some time to think about *your* life in Jesus' name. Remind yourself of John 10:14. You are *known*. Write about that. Do you have that life? If not, it is yours for the taking if you just believe!

The Lord is my shepherd; I shall not want.
PSALM 23:1

CHAPTER 4

PASTURES of the SHEPHERD

Ezekiel 34:11-31

He makes me lie down in green pastures.
He leads me beside still waters.
PSALM 23:2

You had a little teaser in your homework last week when you read Ezekiel 34:1-10. Question 1 on Day 3 brought our attention to the false shepherds about whom Ezekiel writes and to whom Jesus refers, but our focus this week is going to be on the pasture that God provides for His sheep. I sit here typing this just a few days into the COVID-19 pandemonium that has taken our country by storm as the deadly coronavirus continues to wreak havoc across the world. Late last week, stores in the U.S. began running out of toilet paper as widespread panic increased. I have the tendency to laugh and think of inappropriate toilet humor, exchanging funny TP GIFs via text with friends, and I brainstorm about creative alternate TP substitutes should the need arise, but underlying the humor I know that the root cause of this chaos in our country is fear, and *that* we all need to take seriously.

The specific fear we will address this week in our study is the fear of lacking in provisions. As I walked down the aisle at Kroger yesterday, I found a total of twelve boxes of pasta where there once had been hundreds, bread almost down to the crumbs, the meat cases were nearly cleared out, flour, sugar and oil were swiftly disappearing. (The capers for my chicken piccata were fully stocked, though. Imagine that! One fellow shopper found it amusing that I was searching for capers in the first place.) In all seriousness, however, during my relatively short life on this earth, I have never seen anything like the current scene at grocery stores across the nation, but I know there are those still among us who experienced the Great Depression or World War II firsthand and have seen food in short supply. There truly is nothing new under the sun! (Eccles. 1:9). As believers, it is more important than ever that we cling to the truths found in Scripture during times of uncertainty.

A quote that is being widely shared across social media and the internet is one of C. S. Lewis' from his essay 'On Living in an Atomic Age' written in 1948, just three years after the atomic bombs were dropped on Hiroshima and Nagasaki. These two bombings were the decisive and life-altering blow that finally drew the curtains closed on World War II. Lewis' words ring true for any time in history when uncertainty about the future fills the very air we breathe. For the current season, I can substitute 'coronavirus' for 'atomic bomb' in this essay, but at any point in time, we can substitute the current trial in which we find ourselves for 'atomic bomb,' whether it be a natural disaster, war, economic crisis, etc.[1]

> In one way we think a great deal too much of the atomic bomb. 'How are we to live in an atomic age?' I am tempted to reply: 'Why, as you would have lived in the sixteenth century when the plague visited London almost every year, or as you would have lived in a Viking age when raiders from Scandinavia might land and cut your throat any night; or indeed, as you are already living in an age of cancer, an age of syphilis, an age of paralysis, an age of air raids, an age of railway accidents, an age of motor accidents.'

---

1 https://www.thegospelcoalition.org/article/cs-lewis-coronavirus/ Last accessed November 2021.

In other words, do not let us begin by exaggerating the novelty of our situation. Believe me, dear sir or madam, you and all whom you love were already sentenced to death before the atomic bomb was invented: and quite a high percentage of us were going to die in unpleasant ways. We had, indeed, one very great advantage over our ancestors—anesthetics; but we have that still. It is perfectly ridiculous to go about whimpering and drawing long faces because the scientists have added one more chance of painful and premature death to a world which already bristled with such chances and in which death itself was not a chance at all, but a certainty.

This is the first point to be made: and the first action to be taken is to pull ourselves together. If we are all going to be destroyed by an atomic bomb, let that bomb when it comes find us doing sensible and human things—praying, working, teaching, reading, listening to music, bathing the children, playing tennis, chatting to our friends over a pint and a game of darts—not huddled together like frightened sheep and thinking about bombs. They may break our bodies (a microbe can do that) but they need not dominate our minds.

So how do we keep ourselves from letting the fear that we will lack in provisions dominate our minds? We study Scripture and we turn to the Lord in prayer. In times of worry, of anxiety, of chaos and tragedy, we turn to the one place where truth reigns eternal: the Holy Word of God. If we turn to His Word in times of peace and plenty, we will be more prepared when those days of turmoil arise. I encourage you, wherever you are in this season of your life, whether you are basking in a time of plenty or suffocating in a season of drought or sorrow or despair, steep yourself in the truth of God's Word.

This week we will study the promise that God provides pasture for His sheep. He is the Great Shepherd who is *always* with us. 'I myself will be the shepherd of my sheep, and I myself will make them lie down, declares the Lord GOD. I will seek the lost, and I will bring back the strayed, and I will bind up the injured, and I will strengthen the weak, and the fat and the strong I will destroy. I will feed them in justice' (Ezek. 34:15-16).

A key aspect of pasture we must keep in mind is that it provides *rest*. Pasture is provision and rest in the Lord. Jesus said, 'Come to me, all who labor and are heavy laden, and I will give you rest. Take my yoke upon you, and learn from me, for I am gentle and lowly in heart, and you will find rest for your souls.' (Matt. 11:28-29). The Lord *knows* you—He knows where your heart is right now, He knows what fears are drowning out His voice, He knows what rest you need and what is hindering you from finding that rest. May you experience the richness of God's pasture as you seek Him in His Word. You lack nothing because He provides everything.

HOMEWORK & REFLECTION

DAY 1

1. Before digging into Ezekiel 34, we owe it to ourselves to get a basic handle on the context of the book. The prophet Ezekiel was God's spokesman to the exiled people of Judah when they were first deported from Jerusalem to Babylon. His prophetic ministry began a few years later with his first vision in 593 B.C. and concluded in 571 B.C. Chapter 34 was likely written after the fall of Jerusalem and the destruction of the Temple in 586 B.C. There was great confusion and distress during this period in the history of the Jewish people. Their exile was a direct consequence of their unfaithfulness to the Lord. Some of the themes found in the book of Ezekiel are: 1. The restoration of God's people to holiness. 2. The Lord's sovereignty over all. 3. Hope amidst judgment. 4. The promise of a future prince.[2]

---

2   https://www.esv.org/resources/esv-global-study-bible/introduction-to-ezekiel/ Last accessed November 2021.

Read 2 Kings 24:10-17. This is the record of the time during which Ezekiel himself was exiled to Babylon along with the rest of the first wave of deportees from Jerusalem in 597 B.C. Nebuchadnezzar, king of Babylon, captured the city and sent King Jehoiachin and others into captivity. He set up Zedekiah as a puppet king, whose so-called reign would last for the next eleven years until it came to a brutal end with the fall of Jerusalem in 586 B.C. as recorded in 2 Kings 25.

2. Now we are ready to read Ezekiel 34, including verses 1-10. Although the focus of our study will be on verses 11-31, reading the beginning of the chapter will help you understand the context. Take your time. Meditate on each phrase, word and idea. Perhaps it would help you to read it out loud. Study the cross-references in the footnotes of your Bible if you like. Jot down anything that comes to mind as God's Word speaks to you.

....

....

....

....

....

....

DAY 2

1. For today, we're going to look closely at Ezekiel verses 11-16. Go ahead and read those verses and record any initial observations.

....

....

....

....

....

....

2. Now go through and write down all the things that the Lord does
   as a Shepherd. (Hint: find the verbs.)

....

....

....

....

....

....

3. Think about how the Lord as the Shepherd models both authority
   and service. What can you learn from this model?

....

....

....

....

....

....

4. We see how the Lord seeks out and searches for His sheep and
   then He rescues them. He takes care to seek out the scattered.
   Now read Luke 15:4-7 and discuss how Ezekiel 34:12 foreshadows
   the shepherd seeking out the wandering sheep in Jesus' parable.

....

....

....

....

....

....

5. The pastoral imagery of a lush pasture would have been much more meaningful to the audience of the day than it is to most modern readers because the economy in the ancient world of the Bible was agriculturally based. The Lord promises to feed His sheep with *good* pasture and says they will 'lie down in *good* grazing land, and on rich pasture they shall feed…' (v. 14). In Scripture, 'pasture' is often used to signify security and supply.[3] Look at the ways in which the Lord provides security and supply in verses 11-16 and comment on them.

....

....

....

....

....

....

6. What does it look like for you to find 'pasture' in the Lord and in His provisions for your life? Describe the 'pasture' that He has given you. If you struggle to recognize His 'pasture' in your life, write about that.

---

3 *Dictionary of Biblical Imagery,* 'Pasture,' p. 630.

....

....

....

....

....

....

DAY 3

1. Let's turn our attention to Ezekiel 34:16-22. Before anything else, read this section and write down any thoughts you have.

....

....

....

....

....

....

2. Out of His perfect love, the Lord brings judgment on His people. In the time of Ezekiel, a flock would have sheep, but quite often it would also include rams and goats. This is not the same image of sheep and goats found in Matthew 25:31-46 where the sheep are those who are saved and the goats are the unsaved. In Ezekiel 34:17, these animals are simply representing various individuals among the people of God.[4] With that in mind, comment on how the Israelites must be treating one another as revealed in verses 18-19.

....

4 Taylor, John B. *Ezekiel: An Introduction and Commentary*, pp. 221-2.

....

....

....

....

....

3. When the stronger sheep take advantage of their strength, what is the effect on the rest of the flock? How do you think this translates to people? What happens to the pasture that the Lord provides when this happens?

....

....

....

....

....

....

4. Explain how God is righteous in His judgment between the fat and the lean sheep in verses 20-22. Judgment is a difficult topic to discuss, but what would this situation look like if the Lord did *not* judge? Why is judgment *by the Lord* necessary for His people to thrive?

....

....

....

....

....

....

DAY 4

1. There is good news that we will study today! Immediately following His promise of judgment, the Lord makes an amazing promise in verses 23-24. Explain that promise and any of your initial thoughts after you read those verses.

....

....

....

....

....

....

2. Let's take a deeper look at the phrase, 'my servant David,' which regularly refers to the Messiah in Scripture. Read the following Scriptures and record what you discover regarding the Savior who is to come.

- Jeremiah 23:1-6

    ....

    ....

    ....

- Jeremiah 30:8-9

    ....

    ....

    ....

- Ezekiel 37:24-25

....

....

....

- Hosea 3:5

....

....

....

3. Can you see how Jesus probably had Ezekiel 34 in mind in John 10? Look at John 10:14-18 again to remind yourself that Jesus is the Good Shepherd. In His authority, He provided the most amazing act of service and love on your behalf. Write down your thoughts as you look at Ezekiel 34:23-24 alongside John 10:14-18. What type of 'pasture' or provision do you see here?

....

....

....

....

....

....

DAY 5

1. For the last day this week, we are going to close out Ezekiel 34 by studying verses 25-31. Go ahead and read that section and jot down any initial impressions.

....

....

....

....

....

....

2. Read Zechariah 8:12-13. Discuss the idea of peace in Ezekiel and Zechariah as you understand it from these passages.

....

....

....

....

....

....

3. So far we have looked at the pastures that the Lord provides here and now, but this section focuses on pastures that will belong to the children of God in the future. Write down what these pastures look like, according to verses 25-29.

....

....

....

....

....

....

4. Take time to rejoice in the Lord today! Thank Him for what the future holds for you as a believer in Christ. Thank Him for the provisions He has given you today. Meditate on Ezekiel 34:30-31 and Psalm 100 as part of your prayer. Write down your prayer if that helps you focus. It does not matter exactly what this exercise looks like for you—what matters is that you take some time to be with the Lord!

....

....

....

....

....

....

He makes me lie down in green pastures. He leads me beside still waters.

PSALM 23:2

CHAPTER 5

RESTORATION by the SHEPHERD
Psalm 30

He restores my soul.
PSALM 23:3a

The theme of restoration is a prominent thread woven throughout the Bible from beginning to end. God's entire story is one of restoring His creation to what it was meant to be before sin sunk its teeth into the flesh of this world and tried to devour all the goodness that God originally instilled. The objects of restoration within Scripture are wide and varied—slaves are restored to freedom, land is restored to fruitfulness, barren women are restored and become mothers, the Temple is restored after destruction, health is restored from terrible diseases, souls are restored from despair, life itself is restored in resurrection from the dead, the entire earth is restored when Jesus returns again.[1] Our focus this week will primarily be on the restoration of the soul as we see in verse 23a of Psalm 23, but I want you to be acutely aware of the myriad of pictures the Lord gives us of restoration.

My journey through the dark valley of depression is one I hope to never traverse again, but if I do I will cling to the promises of restoration. Since I have now experienced that depth of despair,

---

1 *Dictionary of Biblical Imagery* 'Restore, Restoration,' p. 710.

not only can I look to God's promises, but I can also remember God's grace while I was trying to climb out of the pit. *Remembering God's goodness is of paramount importance to people who are in the throes of suffering of any kind.* One day I was drawn to 1 Peter 5:10, which says, 'And after you have suffered a little while, the God of all grace, who has called you to his eternal glory in Christ, will himself restore, confirm, strengthen, and establish you.' I would like to share with you what I recorded in my journal after meditating on this: *The Lord is restoring my mind. I am fighting daily for His truths to sink in, and in His time they are. I am slowly being granted the ability to see Him more clearly once again. Thank God! I have so deeply missed the clarity of mind that I normally take for granted.* A year and a half after composing that short entry, I am incredibly grateful to have this vivid reminder, penned by my own hand, of what God did for me in the midst of my despair.

We all need restoration in different ways—we need God to rescue us from an array of afflictions and uniquely challenging circumstances. Perhaps you have a teenager with a rebellious heart or a spouse with whom you feel you have nothing in common anymore. You might be in the middle of a horrendous divorce that is tearing your entire family apart. Maybe you are fighting a protracted disease or unrelenting chronic pain, or you recently heard a doctor utter those life-changing words, 'You have cancer.' You may be grieving the loss of someone dear to you—death may have stolen that person from you, or a fractured relationship may have created a divide greater than the Grand Canyon between you. It could be that you gave birth to your infant prematurely and are terrified of what the future holds for your precious little one, or that you are discovering significant developmental delays in your beautiful young child. The astounding truth to which the whole of Scripture attests is that the Lord is in the business of restoring all that is broken! It does not matter if it is a chorus in your life that is slightly out of tune or a dream that has been shattered into a million pieces. The Great Shepherd of our souls rescues us, brings us back to the flock and renews our hearts. This is great reason to praise Him!

Psalm 30 provides a beautiful story of a soul restored as David recounts a time he fell out of favor with the Lord. As he sought the Lord for help, God gloriously turned his 'mourning into dancing' and his sorrow into joy. Every single one of God's children can experience this restoration of the soul for which David praises the Lord in Psalm 30. Remember, He *knows* you and *loves* you. He desires for you to turn to Him so He can lift you up, giving you the gifts of restoration and renewal. His greatest gift of all is that of Jesus, who, through the precious sacrifice of His spotless life for your sinful one, was restored to the Father by rising from the dead. He sits at the right hand of the Father, and not only is He restored, but He is also *exalted!* Look at what Paul teaches in Philippians 2:5-11. As you get ready to start your study of Psalm 30 this week, praise God for what he has given you in Jesus.

Have this mind among yourselves, which is yours in Christ Jesus, who, though he was in the form of God, did not count equality with God a thing to be grasped, but emptied himself, by taking the form of a servant, being born in the likeness of men. And being found in human form, he humbled himself by becoming obedient to the point of death, even death on a cross. Therefore God has highly exalted him and bestowed on him the name that is above every name, so that at the name of Jesus every knee should bow, in heaven and on earth and under the earth, and every tongue confess that Jesus Christ is Lord, to the glory of God the Father.

HOMEWORK & REFLECTION

DAY 1

1. Read slowly through Psalm 30. Compare two or more versions of the psalm (I like the ESV and NIV) to see if that helps to clarify or illuminate any part of it. Meditate on each phrase, word and idea. Use the cross-references in the footnotes of your Bible or create an outline of the psalm if you like. Write down anything that comes to mind as God's Word speaks to you. Remember, sitting with the text like this really helps you own it!

....

....

....

....

....

....

2. We do not know for certain the exact occasion for which David wrote this psalm or the reason for his fall from the Lord's favor at this point in his life, though we know enough of his history to recognize that this song was written as a reflection of his very real life experiences. A vast array of quite poignant emotions is recorded in this psalm. What emotions do you see? What is the overall tone? Do you connect with any of the emotions that David expresses?

....

....

....

....

....

....

3. Look up the word 'restore' in a dictionary and write down the definition. How does this relate to our passage?

....

....

....

....

....

....

DAY 2

1. Turn your focus on Psalm 30:1-3 today. This song begins with words of praise, so let's explore why David is praising God. What image comes to mind when you read the words, 'for you have drawn me up'?

....

....

....

....

....

....

2. What are the various trials from which God has saved David? Do any of these resonate with you?

....

....

....

....

....

....

3. We are going to take some time to explore the theme of restoration in other passages of scripture. Jot down your thoughts as you meditate on these verses.

- Psalm 41:1-3

....

....

....

- Psalm 71:19-21

....

....

....

- Isaiah 41:10

....

....

....

- Isaiah 57:14-21

....

....

....

- Jeremiah 17:14-18

....

....

....

DAY 3

1. For today we will explore verses 4 and 5. David shifts from personal praise of the Lord to enlisting others to join him in his endeavor. It is absolutely beautiful—in verse 4 we get to see how David's heart is so moved by the goodness of the Lord that he wants others to share in that joy and to praise the Lord alongside him. Has worship ever driven you to want to share it with others? What does individual worship look like in your life? What about communal worship?

....

....

....

....

....

....

2. What goes hand in hand with praise (hint: see the second half of v. 4)?

....

....

....

....

....

....

3. What is the reason that David gives in verse 5 for the community of believers to offer praise and thanks to God? What contrasts do you find in his imagery?

....

....

....

....

....

....

4. In light of this idea comment on the following passages.

- Exodus 20:6

  ....

  ....

  ....

- Exodus 34:6-9

  ....

  ....

  ....

- Nehemiah 9:16-17

  ....

  ....

  ....

- Psalm 118:29

  ....

  ....

  ....

- Isaiah 57:15-16 (yes, please revisit this passage!)

  ....

  ....

  ....

- Lamentations 3:22-23

  ....

  ....

  ....

DAY 4

1. Read Psalm 30:6-10. David recounts what happened in his relationship with the Lord. Write down any initial thoughts you have on these verses.

   ....

   ....

   ....

   ....

   ....

   ....

2. Read verse 6 in both the ESV and NIV. Look at the words 'prosperity' in the ESV and 'secure' in the NIV and explain what David is saying here.

....

....

....

....

....

....

3. In the first part of verse 7 David now recognizes why he was prosperous and secure. Who is responsible for this?

....

....

....

....

....

....

4. What happens in the second half of verse 7?

....

....

....

....

....

....

5. It appears that David had become self-reliant as success had seduced him into forgetting his need for God. When he realizes his error, what does he do in verses 8-10?

....

....

....

....

....

....

6. Can you think of a time in your life when you became complacent in your walk with the Lord, content in your circumstances? What happened? How did the Lord draw you out of your complacency?

....

....

....

....

....

....

7. What are some defining characteristics of the lives of people who live independently of God?

....

....

....

....

....

....

DAY 5

1. We will close out our study of Psalm 30 by reading verses 11-12. Read the final verses first and then read the entire psalm straight through. What strikes you?

....

....

....

....

....

....

2. David begins the song with praise and he ends it with praise. Describe the imagery used in verse 11.

....

....

....

....

....

....

3. Can you relate to David here? Can you think of a time when God has turned your mourning into dancing and clothed you with gladness? Are you currently stuck in a holding pattern, waiting and pleading and crying out for restoration? Please explain.

....

....

....

....

....

....

4. What is the end result of the Lord's restoration of David, as we see in verse 12?

....

....

....

....

....

....

5. When the Lord has restored you, how have you responded?

....

....

....

....

....

....

He restores my soul. PSALM **23:3a**

CHAPTER 6

RIGHTEOUSNESS in the SHEPHERD
Romans 4:13–5:2

He leads me in paths of righteousness for his name's sake.
PSALM 23:3b

The words *righteous* and *righteousness* are used roughly 550 times in the Bible, which is about 200 more occurrences than we find for the word *faith*. We know how important *faith* is to the gospel, so this staggering word count for *righteous* should begin to give us an idea of how critical it is as well. Stop for a minute and think of your definition for *righteous*. What does this word mean to you? If you were a child of the 1980s and '90s like yours truly, you might think of someone exclaiming, 'Righteous!' in a *Bill and Ted's Excellent Adventure* sort of way, or maybe you are reminded of Ferris Bueller as described by Grace Wheelberg, Principal Rooney's assistant, 'Oh he's very popular Ed…they all adore him. They think he's a righteous dude.' One definition found on *Urban Dictionary* of this version of *righteous* is: 'Awesome, amazing, cool, exciting, etc. Often associated with surfers.' The slang term even made a comeback in 2003 as a common exclamation by the sea turtles in *Finding Nemo*.

Obviously, the slang expression does not give us a full understanding of what righteous truly means, but it begins to point to it. Righteousness *is* awesome, amazing and cool, but we need to look at a full definition to get a grasp of its robust meaning. The original Greek word for righteousness frequently used by Paul in the New Testament can mean 'righteousness, innocence, justice, justification.'[1] As William Mounce expounds upon this definition, he summarizes that righteousness 'is a gift that we receive from God when we believe, is a present reality in our lives, and is a future hope toward which we aspire.' This week we are going to unpack what this *biblical* righteousness is. When the psalmist writes, 'He leads me in paths of righteousness for his name's sake,' what exactly does that mean?

As it turns out, righteousness is key to understanding our salvation in Jesus Christ, and the passage we will study this week is fundamental to that understanding. Romans 4:13–5:2 is rich and deep, and though we certainly won't have time to explore all the intricacies of it, we can begin to probe its depths. It all begins with faith, so let's start there.

I want you to think of your faith as the vehicle through which you gain the righteousness of Christ. Paul devotes an entire chapter of his letter to the Romans explaining this doctrine to early believers; therefore I have to conclude that it must be of utmost importance! God *declares* you righteous—He alone has the authority to say it is so, to say you are something that you are not. However, He does not *make* you righteous—remember you still sin![2] By *declaring* you righteous through your faith in Christ, He *justifies* you. This is the big, fancy, theological doctrine of Justification by Faith. Don't get hung up in these nerdy words and check out—this will begin to make more sense as we study the Word.

---

1 Mounce, William D., *Mounce's Complete Expository Dictionary of Old & New Testament Words*, pp. 592-5.

2 Kevin Jamison's sermon, 'Faith Alone,' preached on November 15, 2017 at Sojourn East.

Basically, what we have is a philosophical struggle of the Christian life: we now stand before God as righteous because of the righteousness of Jesus—yet we are still sinners and will be until the day we die. What a glorious paradox! We are counted righteous not because of anything we have done other than to *believe* in the life, death and resurrection of Jesus Christ.[3] How can He possibly see us as righteous while we still engage daily in the bitter war with sin?

Here's how:

1. God first *imputes* (or credits) righteousness to us. We are counted perfect *before* we are even good! As Pastor John Piper puts it, God, in His infinite grace, does this before we even take our first baby steps in becoming a 'good' Christian. He does this *through* the vehicle of our faith. [4]

2. God then *imparts* (or gives) to us the fruit of the Spirit. Only after seeing us in the righteousness of Christ—once and for all at the moment we believe in the saving work of Jesus—does God begin to conform us into the image of Jesus as He leads us in paths of righteousness. Righteous works then become proof of our righteous standing in Christ Jesus but they are not the cause of it.[5]

Confusing? Yes! It's okay if it's mind-boggling—this truth should stretch every fiber of your mind as you ponder its depth, significance and beauty. Your faith is the bridge that unifies you to Christ so that when God looks at you He sees your union with Jesus and counts you as righteous because He is gazing upon Jesus' perfect righteousness in your place, all while you are still a sinner. This is the beautiful paradox we will seek to understand in Romans. You will be blessed as you

---

3 Schreiner, Thomas R. *Romans,* pp. 209-44.

4 John Piper's sermon 'Faith and the Imputation of Righteousness,' preached on October 17, 1999, desiringgod.org/scripture/romans/4/messages

5 Grudem, Wayne. *Systematic Theology,* pp. 726-7.

explore the righteousness given *to* you by your Great Shepherd *through* your faith in Jesus. He leads you in paths of righteousness for His name's sake.

HOMEWORK & REFLECTION

DAY 1

1. We will start our study of Romans 4:13–5:2 in the same manner that we used on DAY 1 for each prior passage. I hope you're seeing the pattern in how to begin studying a chunk of Scripture! Read the entire selection straight through and then record anything that comes to mind. Go through it slowly. Read aloud if this helps you.

....

....

....

....

....

....

2. Now go back to Romans 3:9 and begin reading there. Continue to read straight through to 5:2. This will give you a better context for our study of righteousness. Write down any verses that strike you as important or anything that clarifies your understanding. Even take note of what is confusing.

....

....

....

....

....

....

DAY 2

1. Let's dig into Romans 4:13-16 for today. Start by praying that the Lord would open your mind to whatever it is He has to offer you in your time with Him. Read verses 13-16 and then read Genesis 15:1-6. Record your observations of the two passages in light of one another.

....

....

....

....

....

....

2. A common misreading of this section (and others like it) would be to view it through the framework of faith *versus* the law. However, given the entirety of Scripture, we would be more accurate to talk about faith in Jesus as a fulfillment of the law, with faith and the law working in sync with one another rather than in opposition to each other. Comment on the following verses in light of this idea.

- Matthew 5:17

....

....

....

- Romans 3:31

....

....

....

- Galatians 2:21

....

....

....

- Galatians 3:19-22

....

....

....

3. What do you think Paul means when he writes in verse 15 'where there is no law there is no transgression'?

....

....

....

....

....

....

DAY 3

1. Read Romans 4:17-21. Paul discusses Abraham's personal faith more thoroughly in these verses, but he does something interesting at the beginning of them: he focuses on God's character in verse 17. What is the character sketch of God that we receive from this verse?

....

....

....

....

....

....

2. Write down a description of Abraham's faith as you understand it from these verses.

....

....

....

....

....

....

3. What are Abraham's circumstances?

....

....

....

....

....

....

• Despite his circumstances, what happened to his faith, according to Paul?

....

....

....

....

....

....

- When your circumstances have been less than ideal, and maybe even downright impossible, what has happened to your faith? Did it deepen and grow or did you waver and fall on your face? Be honest here! **Strong faith doesn't make Jesus more righteous and weak faith doesn't make Jesus less righteous.** You stand righteous before God because of Jesus' perfect righteousness and absolutely nothing else, certainly not the *strength* of your faith.

....

....

....

....

....

....

4. Read verse 21. How big is your God? Are you fully convinced that God is able to do what He has promised?

....

....

....

....

....

....

For many of us it's easy to believe in the *eternal* promise that we have salvation in Jesus' name, but much harder to have faith in the *immediate* promises concerning the fullness of life *here and now* during our life on earth. Is this a struggle for you? Why or why not?

DAY 4

1. We will focus on Romans 4:22-25 as we continue our study on righteousness. Find all the places in Romans 4 where we see the idea that faith is counted as righteousness. Essentially, the entire chapter is an exposition of Genesis 15:6!

....

....

....

....

....

....

2. Read Romans 3:21-22.

• How is the righteousness of God manifested apart from the law?

....

....

....

....

....

....

• What role do the Law and the Prophets have in the manifest-ation of God's righteousness?

....

....

....

....

....

....

3. Now let's go back to Romans 4:23-24. Why were the words about Abraham's faith being 'counted to him as righteousness' written?

....

....

....

....

....

....

4. Do you identify with these words in your own life? Read verse 24. Do you 'believe in him who raised from the dead Jesus our Lord…'?

....

....

....

....

....

....

5. Read Romans 4:25 and 2 Corinthians 5:21.

- What happens to your sin?

....

....

....

....

....

....

- What happens to Jesus' righteousness?

....

....

....

....

....

....

- How do you process those seemingly impossible truths? Remember from 4:17, this is the God 'who gives life to the dead and calls into existence the things that do not exist.'

....

....

....

....

....

....

DAY 5

Nothing is impossible with God. This passage vividly shows us that truth. God has the unstoppable power and the infinite mercy to place every one of our sins on His perfect, sinless Son, who offered up His very life to make us right with God. The Lord now looks upon His vile, sinful creatures and declares us righteous because our faith in Jesus links us irrevocably to His righteousness. We are clean in His eyes before we can ever be fully clean! As David cried out under the crushing weight of his murderous and adulterous sins, 'Purge me with hyssop, and I shall be clean; wash me, and I shall be whiter than snow,' we can cry the same, in the name of Jesus, and know with full assurance that we are clean (Ps. 51:7). Take time right now to praise God for the righteousness you have in Christ.

1. Read the first two verses of Romans 5. Notice the connecting word *Therefore*. Although there is a chapter break right before this word, Paul's words in chapter 5 go hand in hand with what he wrote in chapter 4.

    ....

    ....

    ....

    ....

    ....

    ....

    - What do we *gain* because of our justification by faith, according to 5:1-2?

      ....

      ....

      ....

      ....

....

....

• What do we *do*, according to 5:2b?

....

....

....

....

....

....

2. Not only do we rejoice because of the right standing we have been given before God, but we are also spurred on to love and do good works because He first loved us. As Pastor Kevin Jamison once said, 'We are not loved because we are good, but hopefully we become good because we experience that we are loved.'[6] Read Philippians 1:9-11, 1 Timothy 6:11-12, 2 Timothy 2:22-25. How do these words resonate with you personally?

....

....

....

....

....

....

The writer of Hebrews gave a benediction to his audience at the end of his letter. Allow me to close our study of the Good Shepherd this

---

6 Kevin Jamison's sermon, 'Faith Alone,' preached on November 15, 2017 at Sojourn East.

week with his words. Let them permeate your soul as you ponder how the Lord leads you in paths of righteousness.

> Now may the God of peace who brought again from the dead our Lord Jesus, the great shepherd of the sheep, by the blood of the eternal covenant, equip you with everything good that you may do his will, working in us that which is pleasing in his sight, through Jesus Christ, to whom be glory forever and ever. Amen.
>
> HEBREWS 13:20-21

He leads me in paths of righteousness for his name's sake.
PSALM 23:3b

CHAPTER 7

SUFFERING as a FOLLOWER of the SHEPHERD
1 Peter 4:12–5:11

Even though I walk through the valley of the shadow of death,
I will fear no evil, for you are with me…

PSALM 23:4a

The valley of the shadow of death. This phrase reverberates deeply with one poignant aspect of our humanity—no human being is exempt from suffering. Every single one of us walks through the valley of the shadow of death at different points throughout our lives. Death cast its dark shadow across life the moment sin entered the world at the Fall of Man. As sons and daughters of Adam and Eve, we live with the ever-present reminder of death every day of our lives. Natural disasters, chronic or terminal medical diseases, stillborn babies, domestic violence, horrific accidents, warfare between nations, estranged relationships, and countless other tragic circumstances prove that this is not the world it once was at the time of creation when 'God saw everything that he had made, and behold, it was very good' (Gen. 1:31). Once Adam and Eve gave themselves over to temptation and disobeyed God, not everything could be 'very good' anymore.

The apostle Paul wrote in Romans 8:22, 'we know that the whole creation has been groaning together in the pains of childbirth until now.' This groaning that Paul is talking about encompasses all of the brokenness we see around us. Sometimes I am just overcome by the

89

sense that *it's not supposed to be this way.* Do you ever feel that? We *should* feel it because the world is no longer the way it was meant to be; it is now in bondage to sin. Paul goes on to say in verse 23 of Romans 8, 'And not only the creation, but we ourselves...groan inwardly as we wait eagerly for adoption as sons, the redemption of our bodies.' All of creation, including us, is waiting for that beautiful day when *everything* will be redeemed.

Why does suffering exist? Humans have been trying to answer this question from the dawn of civilization. Myths have been created in an attempt to make sense of the pain and anguish that pervades this life. In the ancient world, gods and goddesses of various pagan religions were thought to meddle with the lives of humans. These deities were held both in awe and trembling fear due to the power they wielded. Their supposed existence attempted to explain the senseless and unjustifiable suffering that humans experienced, often due to the fleeting whims and desires of the gods. Perhaps one of the most well-known myths is that of the Trojan War, a decade-long siege marked by many battles, deaths and destruction, the result of the skirmish of three Greek goddesses who childishly fought over a golden apple at a wedding feast.[1]

World religions today offer various reasons for suffering. In Hinduism, suffering is closely related to the idea of karma (what goes around comes around), so suffering can be a result of past thoughts and actions either in the current life or a past life. The goal is to try to learn from the suffering and resolve it and hope for a better reincarnation. Buddhists seek to transcend suffering by a process of gradual self-improvement with the end result being a state of enlightenment whereby one is not held captive to anything in this world.

---

1 https://www.theoi.com/articles/what-was-the-cause-of-the-trojan-war/ Last accessed November 2021.

In stark contrast, however, Christianity differs significantly in its consideration of suffering as part of the human experience. Tragedy in this world is not due to the whim of a fickle deity. Pain and sorrow are a reality that cannot be escaped by simply improving oneself. Suffering can be a result of sinful actions or desires, but it can also occur without any seeming rhyme or reason. It can be caused by demonic influences as we see in the case of Job when God allows Satan a degree of access into Job's life and his faith is tested. Suffering can be used by God to sanctify His children, to deepen their faith and conform them more into the image of His Son. The only antidote to suffering is God Himself and His final restoration when Jesus returns. John reports the vision God gave him of this future renewal in the book of Revelation:

> Then I saw a new heaven and a new earth, for the first heaven and the first earth had passed away, and the sea was no more. And I saw the holy city, new Jerusalem, coming down out of heaven from God, prepared as a bride adorned for her husband. And I heard a loud voice from the throne saying, 'Behold, the dwelling place of God is with man. He will dwell with them, and they will be his people, and God himself will be with them as their God. He will wipe away every tear from their eyes, and death shall be no more, neither shall there be mourning, nor crying, nor pain anymore, for the former things have passed away.' And he who was seated on the throne said, 'Behold, I am making all things new.' Also he said, 'Write this down, for these words are trustworthy and true.'

REVELATION 21:1-5

The only way to deal with suffering until that glorious day comes is to bring all of our burdens to the Lord and to seek what Scripture says about the character of God and our right standing before Him as believers in Jesus Christ.

In the Bible, we do not find instructions on how to escape suffering or how to improve our lives so that we might have a better reincarnated life or reach a blissful state of enlightenment. Rather, we find truth. Hard truth. Jesus tells His followers they will suffer tribulation (John 16:33) and they will suffer as the objects of hatred (John 15:19). Do you hear that? As a believer in Christ, suffering is *assured* in your life. There is no escaping it, but there is a right posture to have while enduring it. This posture is what we will be seeking to understand in our study this week. It can be summed up in Peter's words that come straight from our passage:

> Therefore let those who suffer according to God's will entrust their souls to a faithful Creator while doing good.
>
> 1 PETER 4:19

In this one verse there is much to unearth, but for the moment, let me draw your eyes to the word *entrust*. When we find ourselves in any difficult circumstance, whether it be a disagreement with a co-worker or the death of a loved one, we must *entrust* our souls to our great God. Trusting God is key to the posture that we should take while traversing any dark valley.

What exactly do we trust when we say that we trust God? For starters, we trust the words of the Bible inspired by the Lord Himself. We trust that God is the Creator who spoke everything from nothing, who created us from the dust of the earth out of His sheer goodness and knows every hair on our heads. We trust that *all* things work together for our good (Rom. 8:28), even when it seems absolutely impossible that your son's death or your breast cancer or your bipolar disorder or your job loss or your paralysis or your _____ [insert any personal heart-wrenching circumstance] could ever result in your good. Even when these awful realities of life pummel us with the force of a freight train—*even then*—we trust Him.

I do not say this lightly, and I do not pretend to understand the ways of God (Isa. 55:8-9), but He has given us His Word and tells us that we can trust Him. We trust that He is in control, and we cannot ever be snatched from His hand (John 10:29). In Him we are absolutely, unequivocally safe, even in the valley of the shadow of death. As Jesus said to His disciples shortly before His death, 'I have said these things to you, that in me you may have peace. In the world you will have tribulation. But take heart; I have overcome the world' (John 16:33). As we get started for the week, take some time to praise the One who has overcome the world! If you are currently in a season of suffering, may you find renewed strength to carry on, and if you are in a season of rejoicing, may our study of 1 Peter 4 and 5 strengthen you for any difficult times that might lie ahead.

HOMEWORK & REFLECTION

DAY 1

1. I think you know the drill by now. Spend some time asking the Lord to open your heart to what He has for you in this passage. Read our passage for the week, 1 Peter 4:12–5:11, and write down your initial observations. Look for any repeated phrases or ideas, research cross-references, and record your personal thoughts on these words that Peter wrote nearly two thousand years ago.

....

....

....

....

....

....

2. Allow me to give you a brief lesson on the context of 1 Peter. It is a letter believed to have been written by the apostle Peter, while he was in Rome, to the Christians scattered across an area in Asia Minor that was under Roman control (modern day Turkey). It was likely written in the early A.D. 60s during the rule of Emperor Nero, who was a known tyrant and fervent persecutor of Christians. The main theme is to stand firm in the face of persecution as there is hope for believers in Christ who persevere. Peter's purpose is to encourage his brothers and sisters in Christ that they can endure suffering by giving themselves entirely to God.[2]

Now go back and read our passage one more time. Can you understand it a little bit better after learning about the context? Does it change your perspective at all?

....

....

....

....

....

....

DAY 2

1. Our focus today will be on 1 Peter 4:12-19. When Peter writes of the 'fiery trial' in verse 12 he is specifically talking about persecution, but for our purposes as believers, the words can apply to anything that comes into our lives by way of pain *while we are walking in obedience* to the Lord.[3] For what purpose is this fiery trial upon the original readers, according to verse 12?

---

2 https://www.esv.org/resources/esv-global-study-bible/introduction-to-1-peter/ Last accessed November 2021.

3 John Piper's sermon 'Why We Can Rejoice in Suffering' preached on October 23, 1994, desiringgod.org.

....

....

....

....

....

....

2. What does Peter instruct his listeners to do in verse 13 as one response to their suffering?

....

....

....

....

....

....

3. Now read Romans 8:18. What does this verse have in common with 1 Peter 4:13?

....

....

....

....

....

....

4. What does it look like for you to rejoice in your suffering? Give an example if you have one.

....

....

....

....

....

....

5. In any trial we face, the Holy Spirit is with us. We are not alone. Read verse 14. What do you think these words meant to the first-century believers who were hearing them?

....

....

....

....

....

....

- Now read Matthew 5:10. What does Jesus promise to those who are persecuted for the sake of righteousness?

....

....

....

....

....

....

- Have you ever been insulted for the name of Christ? If so, please share your experience.

....

....

....

....

....

....

DAY 3

Let's continue to study 1 Peter 4:12-19.

1. In verses 15-16 Peter contrasts two different types of suffering.
    List those below.

    *   suffering as a _____ or _____ or

        _____ or _____

    *   suffering as a _____

2. For those who suffer as Christians, what does Peter instruct us to
    do in verse 16?

    ....

    ....

    ....

    ....

    ....

    ....

    *   What does this look like in your life?

        ....

        ....

....

....

....

....

3. Verses 17-18 can be difficult to understand. What do you make of these verses when you read them? See also Proverbs 11:31, from which Peter is quoting in verse 18.

....

....

....

....

....

....

As commentator David Guzik explains, 'Now is our time of *fiery trial*; the ungodly will have their fire later. The fire we endure now purifies us; the fire the ungodly will endure will punish them. Yet we always remember that there is never any punishment from God for us in our sufferings, only purification. For the Christian, the issue of *punishment* was settled once and for all at the cross, where Jesus endured all the punishment the Christian could ever face from God.'[4]

4. What is the connecting word used in verse 19?

....

....

....

....

---

4 https://enduringword.com/bible-commentary/1-peter-4/ Last accessed November 2021.

....

....

- After all that Peter has discussed about suffering as a believer in verses 12-18, what does he conclude is the posture that we should take?

....

....

....

....

....

....

- The suffering Peter is speaking of is according to whose will?

....

....

....

....

....

....

- Why do you think Peter refers to God here as 'Creator'?

....

....

....

....

....

....

- Our posture does not stop with trusting in God. What are we to do while we trust? (Hint: read the second half of verse 19).

....

....

....

....

....

....

5. What is your personal experience with trusting God in the midst of suffering?

....

....

....

....

....

....

6. What type of witness do Christians give the world when we continue to *do good* while we are suffering? Do you have any examples from your own life or the lives of others that you know?

....

....

....

....

....

....

DAY 4

We are switching gears a little bit today. In light of the suffering that Peter's brothers and sisters are enduring, he provides instructions to the leaders on how to shepherd God's flock. Read 1 Peter 5:1-4.

1. How does Peter describe himself in verse 1? How *could* he have described himself?

    ....

    ....

    ....

    ....

    ....

    ....

2. When Peter wrote these words, he probably thought back on the personal commission that Jesus gave him before He ascended into heaven. Read John 21:15-17. What strikes you about these verses?

    ....

    ....

    ....

    ....

    ....

    ....

3. How are the elders instructed to shepherd the flock in verses 2-3?

    ....

    ....

    ....

    ....

....

....

4. What will happen in the future, according to verse 4?

....

....

....

....

....

....

5. Read the following verses and take note of the adjectives used for the Shepherd in each.

• John 10:11

....

....

....

• Hebrews 13:20-21

....

....

....

• 1 Peter 5:4

....

....

....

Warren Wiersbe writes, 'Jesus Christ is the *Good* Shepherd who died for the sheep (John 10:11), the *Great* Shepherd who lives for the sheep (Heb. 13:20-21), and the *Chief* Shepherd who comes for the sheep (1 Pet. 5:4).'[5]

DAY 5

We will close out our study of suffering today. Begin by prayerfully reading 1 Peter 5:5-11.

1. After exhorting the elders in the previous verses, Peter has brief instructions for those under their leadership in the first half of verse 5. What does he instruct them to do?

    ....

    ....

    ....

    ....

    ....

    ....

2. In the second half of verse 5 he broadens his instructions to include all believers. What is his instruction to 'all of you'? What imagery does he use in verse 5 and how does that image help you better understand what he is saying?

    ....

    ....

    ....

    ....

    ....

    ....

---

5   Wiersbe, Warren. *Be Hopeful,* p. 148.

3. Look at verses 5, 6 and 7 together. What do you think Peter means when he says, 'God opposes the proud but gives grace to the humble'?

....

....

....

....

....

....

4. Read Proverbs 3:34. What is the importance of humility in the life of a believer? How is this counterintuitive in our culture today?

....

....

....

....

....

....

5. Read verses 8-9. We must be 'sober-minded' and recognize Satan's presence in the world.

- What metaphor does Peter use in verse 8 for the Devil? What do you think he means by this?

    ....

    ....

    ....

- What are we to do in the face of Satan's opposition to the kingdom of God? (See also Ephesians 6:10-20)

    ....

....

....

6. What encouragement can we gain from fellow believers who are suffering?

....

....

....

....

....

....

7. And now to the glorious promise in verse 10 which leads to the praise in verse 11. Record what will most certainly happen 'after you have suffered a little while' (which may feel like a *long while* in our human understanding of time).

....

....

....

....

....

....

No believer in Jesus Christ suffers alone. The Holy Spirit is within us and will never leave us. We can cast our anxieties on the Lord and entrust our souls to Him. He is the Good Shepherd who died for us, the Great Shepherd who lives for us and the Chief Shepherd who comes for us. 'To him be the dominion forever and ever. Amen.' (1 Pet. 5:11)

Even though I walk through the valley of the shadow of death, I will fear no evil, for you are with me…

PSALM 23:4a

CHAPTER 8

COMFORT in the SHEPHERD
Isaiah 40

… your rod and your staff, they comfort me.

Psalm 23:4b

I find myself putting pen to paper in a bizarre time in world history. As I mentioned earlier, the COVID-19 pandemic has swept the world, striking fear into the hearts of countless people as the uncertainty of the situation perseveres. Recommendations and rules are changing daily, economies have all but shut down, hundreds of thousands have died at this point, medical masks are the new fashion, job loss is rampant, depression and anxiety have ramped up, there is a genuine concern of an increased suicide rate due to the emotional toll of the pandemic, and the 'normal' tragedies of the world unrelated to this virus are still occurring at their regular rate. It is bringing many people to their knees. While some are questioning, 'How could a God exist who allows this type of suffering to happen?', others are turning to God for comfort and drawing companions with them along the way. This is not a novel phenomenon. Suffering has been known to elicit these types of responses throughout the history of mankind, and it will continue to evoke them when the memory of the disruptive coronavirus is hazy and distant.

One YouTube video that recently went viral is called 'The UK Blessing,'[1] and it had over two million views after just one week of being posted. In

---

1   https://youtu.be/PUtll3mNj5U Last accessed November 2021.

the video, you encounter a mosaic of believers, representing sixty-five churches of various denominations across the UK, coming together to sing a blessing over their nation. Our friends across the pond are singing a song written by Kari Jobe of Elevation Worship called 'The Blessing,' and I would like to share the lyrics that have inspired hope and provided global comfort during this crisis:[2]

The Lord bless you
And keep you
Make His face shine upon you
And be gracious to you
The Lord turn His
Face toward you
And give you peace

Amen, amen, amen
Amen, amen, amen
Amen, amen, amen
Amen, amen, amen

May His favor be upon you
And a thousand generations
And your family and your children
And their children, and their children

May His presence go before you
And behind you, and beside you
All around you, and within you
He is with you, He is with you

In the morning, in the evening
In your coming, and your going
In your weeping, and rejoicing
He is for you, He is for you

He is for you, He is for you
He is for you, He is for you
He is for you, He is for you

Amen, amen, amen
Amen, amen, amen

The first time I watched 'The UK Blessing,' tears trickled down my face as I pondered the powerful implications of these saints coming together in worship to praise the one, true God while they sought to speak words of blessing and comfort to their nation. The comfort doesn't come from the singers themselves; rather the comfort comes from the truths found in Scripture. The comfort comes from God Himself. Everything they sing is from truth found within the Bible. The Lord blesses us, He keeps us, He shines His face upon us, He is gracious to us, He turns His face to us, and He gives us peace (Num. 6:24-26). His favor is upon us to the thousandth generation (Exod. 20:6). He goes before us and behind us, surrounding us with love (Pss. 34:7, 139:5). He dwells within us and He is with us by the power of the Holy Spirit (1 Cor. 3:16, Eph. 3:17). At *all* times—morning and evening, coming and going, weeping and rejoicing—He is *for* us. *Always.* (Rom. 8:31-39). The Lord will never leave us or forsake us, as we read in Hebrews 13:5. He is our comfort.

Isaiah 40 is one of the most beautiful passages of Scripture that deals with comfort in times of distress. We will dig deeply into it as we seek the Lord and begin to understand better how we can find the comfort we need in Him. Hopefully you will understand why David was able to write the words, 'your rod and your staff, they comfort me,' hundreds of years before Isaiah prophesied to the divided kingdom of Israel. Isaiah knew God's Word spoken through David's poetry, and he understood why the rod and staff of God the Shepherd provide comfort to His children.

Isaiah was faithful to the Lord during a time of great unfaithfulness in the history of Israel, and God entrusted Isaiah to proclaim words that would provide comfort to His people in a time of great turmoil and uncertainty. The main idea of Isaiah 40 is that there is hope *for those who wait on the Lord (v. 31)*, and comfort can be found in *looking forward* to that hope while *remembering* God's character, strength, power and promises. Maybe this is why 'The UK Blessing' resonated in the hearts of so many people during COVID-19. The lyrics rest in God's promises, *looking forward* in hope and *remembering* His goodness. As you study Isaiah's words that were written about 700 years before the birth of Jesus, I pray that you will find comfort in the Lord, because as the prophet wrote, 'the word of our God will stand forever' (Isa. 40:8).

HOMEWORK & REFLECTION

DAY 1

Let's start today in prayer. Take a few minutes to sit still with the Lord and invite Him into your study and into your heart as you open His Word and seek to know Him better.

1. I'm going to give you a brief history lesson before you read our passage for the week. Having this context will greatly help you understand Isaiah's words.

As I previously mentioned, the book of Isaiah was written about 700 years before Jesus in the late eighth and early seventh centuries B.C., a couple of hundred years after Israel had been divided into the Northern Kingdom (Israel) and the Southern Kingdom (Judah) in 930 B.C. Isaiah prophesied to both Israel and Judah during the Assyrian invasion, in which Israel fell to Assyria in 722 B.C. It would be another century and a half before Judah falls to Babylon (586 B.C.), but Isaiah speaks directly into the events surrounding the Assyrian invasion as well as distant events that would come to pass with the Babylonian exile.

The first thirty-nine chapters of Isaiah are primarily doom and gloom as God uses Isaiah as the mouthpiece from which He declares judgment on His wayward people. Time and again in the Old Testament we see God's chosen ones turn away from Him. The time has come for God to finally hand them over to their enemies. Chapters 1–39 have been referred to as the 'Book of Judgment.' However, we encounter hope in chapter 40, which opens the second section of Isaiah (chapters 40–66), also known as the 'Book of Comfort.' In God's perfect justice, He still loves His rebellious children and provides them comfort and hope. The events of chapter 40 itself come to pass over 100 years after Isaiah wrote the chapter. God is providing hope for His people who will be exiled from their beloved homeland at the hands of the Babylonian Empire.

2. Now take plenty of time to read Isaiah 40 from start to finish. Sit with the text. Read it several times if you can. Take note of phrases that sound familiar and of anything that confuses you. Look for patterns and repeated words or ideas. Write down your reflections in the margins of your Bible or in the space below.

....

....

....

....

....

....

DAY 2

1. Our focus today will be on verses 1-11 of Isaiah 40. Read that section and jot down any initial observations.

....

....

....

....

....

....

2. Read 2 Chronicles 36:15-21. Imagine yourself to be a Jewish
   person from Jerusalem at the time of its capture and you are
   part of the contingent sent off to Babylon. You have now lived
   in exile for over a decade. What might the words that Isaiah
   wrote over a hundred years earlier in 40:1-2 mean to you in
   your suffering?

....

....

....

....

....

....

3. Look closely at Isaiah 40:3-5. Now read John 1:19-28. If verses 1-2
   gave hope and comfort to the exiles for the near future, what
   do the words of verses 3-5 provide?

....

....

....

....

....

....

4. What imagery do we see in verses 6-8?

....

....

....

....

....

....

• What does this picture reveal about people?

....

....

....

....

....

....

• What does it reveal about God?

....

....

....

....

....

....

• Read 1 Peter 1:23-25. What do Peter's words tell us about people who believe in Jesus?

....

....

....

....

....

....

5. Read verses 9-11. Discuss the contrasting characteristics of God recorded in verses 10-11.

....

....

....

....

....

....

DAY 3

1. Beginning back in verse 9, Isaiah starts expounding upon the greatness of God. Keep that in mind as you start your study today by reading Isaiah 40:12-17. What is Isaiah getting at in these verses?

....

....

....

....

....

....

2. What literary tool does he use in verses 12-14? (Hint: look at the punctuation.) How might it be helpful to Isaiah's readers?

....

....

....

....

....

....

3. Now read Romans 11:33-36 and comment on how these verses relate to the passage in Isaiah.

....

....

....

....

....

....

4. What do verses 15-17 say about the nations in comparison to God?

....

....

....

....

....

....

5. How can these verses bring comfort?

....

....

....

....

....

....

• Bible teacher Warren Wiersbe once said, 'If you look at God through your circumstances, He will seem very small and far away, but if by faith you look at your circumstances through God, He will draw very near and reveal His greatness to you.'[3] Can you think of a time in your life when you were comforted as you remembered how infinitely great God is?

....

....

....

....

....

....

• Isaiah 55:8-9 says, 'For my thoughts are not your thoughts, neither are your ways my ways, declares the LORD. For as the heavens are higher than the earth, so are my ways higher than your ways and my thoughts than your thoughts.' Do these words bring you comfort, or do you struggle with them? Be honest here!

---

3 Wiersbe, Warren. *Be Comforted,* p. 132.

....

....

....

....

....

....

DAY 4

1. We pick up right where we left off yesterday. Begin your time with the Lord today by reading Isaiah 40:18-26. What ideas are continued on from the previous verses we have studied?

....

....

....

....

....

....

2. The book of Job gives us a portrait of intense suffering. It teaches us that although we cannot understand the suffering in this world, we can trust in the God who holds the universe together. It is by trusting Him that we can find comfort, which is what Isaiah is writing about as well.

   • Read Job 38. What are the similarities of this passage to Isaiah 40:12-26?

   ....

   ....

....

....

....

....

- Read Job 42:1-3. Can you relate to Job's words to the Lord? Explain.

....

....

....

....

....

....

- Read Job 42:4-6. Have you ever needed to repent like this? What did it look like? What happened after you repented? Do you need to repent now? Take time to pray and talk to God.

....

....

....

....

....

....

DAY 5

1. We will close out our study of Isaiah 40 by exploring verses 27-31. Go ahead and read these verses now, writing down anything that

stands out to you.

....

....

....

....

....

....

2. What is the complaint of God's people in verse 27?

....

....

....

....

....

....

3. Now let's look at Isaiah's inspired answer to this complaint. Read verses 28-31.

   • How is the Lord described in verse 28?

   ....

   ....

   ....

   ....

   ....

   ....

- Of all the names for Yahweh, why do you think that Isaiah uses 'Creator' here?

  ....

  ....

  ....

  ....

  ....

  ....

- What does He give, according to verse 29?

  ....

  ....

  ....

  ....

  ....

  ....

- *Who* does He renew in verse 31? Do you think this includes every Jew taken into captivity?

  ....

  ....

  ....

  ....

  ....

  ....

4. Take the time to write down verse 31 in the space below. Ponder the imagery used. Do you personally find encouragement in these words?

....

....

....

....

....

....

5. Now spend some time with the Lord in prayer. Praise Him for being so very great and loving. Thank Him for what He revealed to you in Isaiah 40. Thank Him for His comfort and care in times of distress. If you are struggling to feel His presence in your life, tell Him about that. Ask Him to reveal more of Himself and to draw you near to Him.

... your rod and your staff, they comfort me.
Psalm 23:4b

CHAPTER 9

PREPARATION and BLESSING by the SHEPHERD

John 14

You prepare a table before me in the presence of my enemies, you anoint my head with oil; my cup overflows.

PSALM 23:5

As we dwelled upon the magnificent comfort that God provides in our study of Isaiah 40, we were reminded of Jesus' coming, of the fact that God's Word is imperishable, and that the Lord's greatness is beyond the scope of our comprehension. As believers in Jesus Christ, we find great comfort in the Lord who renews our strength when we are struggling. We discover comfort in the words of Jesus, 'Let not your hearts be troubled. Believe in God; believe also in me. In my Father's house are many rooms. If it were not so, would I have told you that I go to prepare a place for you?' These sweet words of promise are the opening lines of John 14, which we will study today.

I remember so vividly preparing a place for my firstborn child nearly fourteen years ago before I had ever met her face to face. As Brian and I painted the nursery one of my favorite shades of green, chose complementary pink and cream drapes and bedding in a soft toile pattern, browsed the aisles of Babies R Us to try to choose a crib and bedroom furniture that would withstand the test of time, and hung beautiful white shelves solely for the sake of decorating purposes, my heart absolutely swelled with love. Sometimes I felt so caught up with love for this unborn child relentlessly kicking the back of my ribcage that I felt I would burst. I spent hours upon hours preparing her room for the day we would bring her home, and I loved every minute of it.

If I could so lovingly prepare a place for my child in our home, imagine how much more love our perfect Lord has as He prepares a place for us. We terribly *im*perfect human beings possess the inordinate ability to lavish our love in preparation and anticipation as we await the arrival of new babies, an elderly parent, foster children, missionary friends and out of town guests. If we can do this so well, imagine what Jesus is capable of! He is preparing a place for you and for me, and we will be more than guests of honor when we are in His house. We will be home!

And if this blessing were not enough, *our cup overflows*, as David wrote in Psalm 23. The blessings of the Lord are too great to number and they are scattered throughout Scripture, so we will focus our study on John 14, reveling in the blessings we have in the promises of Jesus, in the amazing work God has for us, and in the Holy Spirit that dwells within us.

The fourteenth chapter of John is part of the 'Upper Room Discourse,' which spans chapters 13-17. We are taken into the hidden upper room where Jesus is spending His final hours during the Last Supper with the disciples. As we enter into this intimate scene in chapter 13, Jesus shows His disciples what true love and servant leadership look like as He washes their feet. Heartbreakingly, He then reveals that one of them will betray Him. After Judas departs, Jesus mysteriously speaks of the Son of Man being glorified, and then He commands them to love one another as He has loved them. He says, 'By this all people will know that you are my disciples, if you have love for one another' (13:35). Peter asks where Jesus is going, and Jesus replies that he cannot follow Him there. Peter brazenly declares, 'Lord, why can I not follow you now? I will lay down my life for you' (13:37). Jesus gently tells Peter that he will deny Him three times. Immediately after this devastating revelation, as Peter is surely reeling from these words, chapter 14 begins and Jesus says, 'Let not your hearts be troubled.'

Just a few paragraphs ago I called these 'sweet words of promise,' and that they most certainly are, but when we look at the context of the passage, we see a depth that we don't get at first glance, especially if we do not look at the part of the scene that comes immediately before. As we study this chapter, we would do well to remember that Jesus is preparing for imminent torture and death on the cross. Soon He will be praying in the garden, sweating drops of blood because His soul is so deeply troubled (Mark 14:32-34),[1] and yet He is comforting his disciples. Think about that! As Jesus is enduring the most difficult hours of His life, He is assuring those that He loves that they need not be troubled. He spends His final moments blessing those whom He holds most dear. Let's take the time to drink deeply of the words that pour forth from Jesus' lips in John 14 and discover the beauty of His promises. Pray that the Lord would bless your time in His Word and that you would draw closer to Him through your study this week. May you be blessed as you see how the Lord is preparing a place for *you*. In Jesus Christ, your cup surely overflows.

HOMEWORK & REFLECTION

DAY 1

1. You've got this! Open your Bible to John 14 and bask in it. Pray to the Lord and ask Him to bless your time in the Word. Read the chapter thoroughly, taking your time. Read it aloud if that helps you. Write down anything that comes to mind in the space

---

1   Sweating blood, or hematidrosis, is a rare but scientifically documented physiological response thought to be related to extreme stress. https://www.webmd.com/a-to-z-guides/hematidrosis-hematohidrosis#1 Last accessed November 2021.

below—confusing parts, beautiful parts, patterns, repeated words, etc.

....

....

....

....

....

....

2. If time permits, read the entire Upper Room Discourse, chapters 13-17. It will give you greater understanding as you grasp the full context of this section of John.

DAY 2

1. Let's begin today by reading John 14:1-4. Do you find comfort in these verses? Are any of these words difficult for you?

....

....

....

....

....

....

2. Look up John 12:27, 13:21 and Mark 14:32-36. The word *troubled* is used in all three of these references. Write down your thoughts as you think about what Jesus is going through and what He is saying to His disciples in 14:1.

....

....

....

....

....

....

3. Although verse 2 has historically been misunderstood at times, the 'house of my Father' means the place where God dwells, and 'rooms' comes from the Greek word which means *rooms, abiding places*.[2] In some older translations, the word 'mansions' was used instead of 'rooms,' and that has led some to the erroneous belief that good Christians will have their own mansions one day in heaven. Though we do not know exactly what our places that Jesus is preparing will look like, we can rest assured they will all be beautiful and amazing. However, we should not be expecting a personal mansion!

- How do you think the disciples felt when Jesus comforted them with these words?

....

....

....

....

....

....

- How do you feel when you think about Jesus preparing a place for *you*?

....

....

---

2 Wiersbe, Warren. *Be Transformed*, p. 34.

....

....

....

....

4. What is Jesus' promise in verse 3?

....

....

....

....

....

....

5. What do you think He means in verse 4?

....

....

....

....

....

....

DAY 3

1. As we get started today, please read John 14:5-11. Yesterday's final question was a bit of a cliffhanger. Go back and review that question. Now look at what Thomas asks in verse 5. Why do you think the disciples do not understand?

....

....

....

....

....

....

2. Discuss Jesus' answer to Thomas in verse 6.

....

....

....

....

....

....

3. Read verse 7. The translation can be a little confusing because it sounds like Jesus is accusing Thomas of not knowing Him in the first half of the verse. In reality the words can be translated, 'If you know me, you will know my Father also' or 'If you have known me, you will know my Father also.'[3] What promise is Jesus giving His disciples here?

....

....

....

....

....

....

3 *ESV* footnote for John 14:7.

4. There is still great confusion among the disciples. Read verses 8-11.

    •   What does Philip's inquisitive statement in verse 8 reveal about their understanding?

    ....

    ....

    ....

    ....

    ....

    ....

    •   What do you think Jesus is saying in His answer in verses 9-11?

    ....

    ....

    ....

    ....

    ....

    ....

    •   Refer back to John 10:38. What similarities and differences do you find between these two passages?

    ....

    ....

    ....

    ....

    ....

    ....

DAY 4

1. We will read John 14:12-24 today. Read these verses and record what you think is the main gist of this section.

....

....

....

....

....

....

2. In verses 12-14, what does Jesus say about those who believe in Him? Take time to praise God for this tremendous blessing.

....

....

....

....

....

....

3. *Why* will Jesus do 'whatever you ask in my name'?

....

....

....

....

....

....

4. What is the natural outcome for those who love Jesus, according to verses 15, 21 and 23?

....

....

....

....

....

....

• This does *not* mean believers will keep His commands *perfectly*—while in our earthly bodies we will always be enticed by sin. Read Galatians 5:16-26 and comment on how Paul's words expand your understanding of what Jesus is saying in this section of John.

....

....

....

....

....

....

5. How are we able to keep Jesus' commands? (Hint: What does He promise in verses 16-17? This is another one of our great blessings in Jesus.)

....

....

....

....

....

....

* Do you find it a struggle to keep in step with the Spirit, as Paul
  talked about in Galatians?

....

....

....

....

....

....

6. We continue to see confusion among the disciples. What does
   Judas (not Iscariot) ask in verse 22 and how does Jesus respond
   in verses 23-24?

....

....

....

....

....

....

DAY 5

1. It's time to close out our study of John 14. Don't rush through today's
   work though! There is much to be unearthed. Read verses 25-31 and
   comment on how Jesus wraps up this portion of His discussion.

....

....

....

....

....

....

2. What does Jesus say that the Holy Spirit will do in verse 26?

....

....

....

....

....

....

3. In verse 27 we find another beautiful blessing resulting from being one with Christ. What do you think Jesus means in this verse?

....

....

....

....

....

....

4. If God is in Jesus and Jesus is in God, and all things were made through Jesus (Col. 1:15), what do you think He means when He says that 'the Father is greater than I'? See Philippians 2:5-11 to help you with this answer.

....

....

....

....

....

....

5. According to verse 29, why is Jesus telling His disciples these things that they cannot fully grasp at the present time?

....

....

....

....

....

....

6. What does verse 30 reveal about Satan? How can we be comforted in this?

....

....

....

....

....

....

7. Why is Jesus obedient to the Father, according to verse 31? What is the result? Look back at 13:31 and 14:13.

....

....

....

....

....

....

• What happens when we are obedient to the Father?

....

....

....

....

....

....

Take time to praise the Lord for sending Jesus, who is preparing a place for you and has not left you alone in this world. Thank Him for the love He showers upon you as He prepares for you to one day come home. Thank Him for the ways in which your cup overflows with blessings. Ask Him to give you eyes to see Him more clearly and to experience the comfort He has to offer.

You prepare a table before me in the presence of my enemies; you anoint my head with oil; my cup overflows.

PSALM 23:5

CHAPTER 10

ETERNAL HOPE in the SHEPHERD

Revelation 21:1–22:5

Surely goodness and mercy shall follow me all the days of my life, and I shall dwell in the house of the Lord forever.

PSALM 23:6

'If I find in myself a desire which no experience in this world can satisfy, the most probable explanation is that I was made for another world.' C. S. Lewis wrote these words in his masterpiece *Mere Christianity*. Can you relate? Are there areas in your life in which you feel utterly unsatisfied? My guess is that your answer is a resounding yes, because the truth is, you were made for another world! Are you unsatisfied with your marriage or lack thereof, or with your job— your duties both inside and outside of your home? Are you tired of the suffering that afflicts your loved ones and fills the newsfeeds every day? Are you weary from parenting a rebellious child or caring for an aging parent? Does your life feel like a reenactment of *Groundhog Day*?[1] Is the daily grind dragging you down? Do you feel guilty for acknowledging this lack of satisfaction?

If so, you are not alone—but there is hope! That hope lies in Jesus Christ. My prayer for you this week is that you will grasp hard and firm to the promises held in Scripture, most notably to the promise that if you are one with Christ, you will dwell with the Lord forever.

---

1 *Groundhog Day*, the 1993 comedy film starring Bill Murray.

We will study this eternal hope and promise through the words of Revelation 21:1–22:5.

Looking back at my battle with depression, in God's grace, the experience revealed to me my own lack of satisfaction and longing for more. At the time, I was profoundly disheartened by the struggles in my personal life, both physical and emotional, and also overwhelmed with the sadness I saw in the world around me. I felt as if no one really knew me or understood me, including my own husband. Do you know what the most effective tool in pulling me up and out of the pit was? The Word of God. Don't get me wrong—it was not the *only* tool that the Lord gave me to fight the disease, but it was the most important one.[2]

One sermon I heard preached during that time was titled 'Kiss the Wave,'[3] and the name was based on Charles Spurgeon's quote 'I have learned to kiss the wave that throws me against the Rock of Ages.' You see, just like *every* other human, Spurgeon was pummeled by his own share of waves that threatened to take him under. He faced difficulty and opposition in his ministry at times and suffered from several physical ailments as well as pain from those conditions that hindered his ability to preach. His devoted wife Susannah became chronically ill in her thirties and lived much of the remainder of her life bedridden. Spurgeon himself battled depression, and at one point he delivered a lecture to his students

---

2 It is critically important that people suffering from depression and other mood disorders get the full complement of help they need. God's Word speaks truth and we absolutely *must* steep ourselves in it, but we must also remember that we might not *instantly* be healed when we turn to the Bible. In fact, for many who suffer, it may take months or years to heal. Other modalities of treatment that God provides to be used in addition to His Word include (but are not limited to) reputable counseling, physical activity and antidepressant medications. Any or all of these can be used in combination, but immersion in the Bible is of utmost importance.

3 Kyle Idleman's sermon 'Kiss the Wave' preached at Southeast Christian Church on November 4, 2018.

titled 'The Minister's Fainting Fits.'[4] In the lecture he told them, 'Knowing by most painful experience what deep depression of spirit means, being visited therewith at seasons by no means few or far between, I thought it might be consolatory to some of my brethren if I gave my thoughts thereon, that younger men might not fancy that some strange thing had happened to them when they became for a season possessed by melancholy; and that sadder men might know that one upon whom the sun has shone right joyously did not always walk in the light.'[5]

Spurgeon learned to 'kiss the wave' that caused him to crash into God out of desperation. Teary-eyed, I listened as the preacher reminded me of the truth: *one day the waves will stop.* The book of Revelation gives us a divine picture of that day, but until it comes to pass, I was reminded of 1 Peter 4:12-13, which we studied several weeks ago. Let's look at Peter's words once again, 'Dear friends, do not be surprised at the fiery ordeal that has come on you to test you.. But rejoice inasmuch as you participate in the sufferings of Christ, so that you may be overjoyed when his glory is revealed.' (NIV)

As we study Revelation 21–22, I pray that you will be overjoyed with the prospect of this future day, because no matter what happens, *it is coming.* And on that day, all the waves that knock you sideways and threaten to drown you in chaos will completely cease. As God declares from the throne,

> 'Behold, the dwelling place of God is with man. He will dwell with
> them, and they will be his people, and God himself will be with them

---

4 Reeves, Michael. *Did You Know That Charles Spurgeon Struggled With Depression?* Feb. 24, 2018. *https://www.crossway.org/articles/did-you-know-that-charles-spurgeon-struggled-with-depression/* Last accessed November 2021.

5 Spurgeon, C. H. *Lectures to My Students, Addresses Delivered to the Students of the Pastors' College, Metropolitan Tabernacle*, vol. 1, p. 167.

as their God. He will wipe away every tear from their eyes, and death shall be no more, neither shall there be mourning, nor crying, nor pain anymore, for the former things have passed away.' (Rev. 21:3-4).

We will surely 'dwell in the house of the Lord forever' (Ps. 23:6). On that day when we finally get to see the Lord face to face, we will be immersed in complete understanding—wholly surrounded by the perfect love of God. There has never been a day in your life that the Lord has not known *you* fully, but one day you will have the pleasure of knowing *Him* fully. When you dwell with the Lord you will forever reside in the place of full knowledge.[6] As Paul says in 1 Corinthians 13:12, 'For now we see in a mirror dimly, but then face to face. Now I know in part; then I shall know fully, even as I have been fully known.' Take time to open your heart to the Lord in prayer as you sit down to learn from His Word this week.

HOMEWORK & REFLECTION
DAY 1

1. You deserve a decent introduction to the Book of Revelation if I am going to ask you to do an in-depth study of chapters 21–22! In all honesty, I come before this book with a bit of fear and trembling because it is—well—it's Revelation! This totally unique book of the Bible falls into the category of apocalyptic literature, which is prophecy of the end times. It contains both prose and poetry and is recorded as a series of visions. These visions were given to the apostle John (who also wrote the fourth Gospel as well as the letters 1, 2, and 3 John) by Jesus Himself toward the end of John's life. It is believed that he documented the visions while he was in exile on the island of Patmos in the Aegean Sea in the mid-nineties. John addressed the book to 'the seven churches that are in Asia' but its message is important for all believers.

---

6 Jonathan Pennington's sermon 'Hoping in Heaven: The First Five Minutes After Death' preached for Sojourn East on May 10, 2020 and shared on https://youtu. be/5gJUhxOV_d8 Last accessed November 2021.

Revelation comes from the Greek word *apokalypsis* which simply means 'unveiling' or 'revealing.' The book reveals the spiritual war that is occurring behind the curtain of human awareness. The church is in one corner of the ring while Satan and his minions are in the other, but the church has the upper hand because Jesus has decisively won the victory through His death and resurrection. Although that final victory has been won, the church 'continues to be assaulted by the dragon, in its death-throes'[7] through persecution, heresy and materialism. The boxing ring of the earth is full of suffering, to which we can certainly attest. The visions of Revelation affirm Christ's victory and encourage believers to endure earthly suffering until a new world order will be ushered in.

Chapters 21:1–22:5 give us a glimpse of that new world order. And although we only understand in part right now, we are assured that we will see the Lord face to face and understand in full on that great day. Let's open our Bibles and get a peek of what is in store for us. We are privileged to have a small window into the reality of our eternal hope.

2. Do the same thing for this passage as you have for the past eight. Pray. Read Revelation 21:1–22:5. Write down anything that strikes your fancy, verses that confuse you (it's okay if there are a lot of them!), repetitive words, themes, etc. Take your time!

....

....

....

....

....

....

---

7 https://www.esv.org/resources/esv-global-study-bible/introduction-to-revelation/ Last accessed November 2021.

DAY 2

1. Read verses 1-4. We'll start off easy. Describe what John saw in verses 1-2.

....

....

....

....

....

....

2. Note that throughout Scripture, the word *heaven* is used in three ways: 1. the earth's atmosphere, what we think of as blue sky, 2. outer space, what we think of as the night sky, 3. the place where God lives in glory.[8] Comment on the following cross references in light of verse 1:

- Psalm 102:25-27

....

....

....

....

....

....

- Isaiah 65:17-19

....

....

---

8 Guzik, David. *The Enduring Word Bible Commentary* https://enduringword.com/bible-commentary/revelation-21/ Last accessed November 2021.

....

....

....

....

- 2 Peter 3:12-13

....

....

....

....

....

....

3. What does the voice from the throne declare in verses 3-4?

....

....

....

....

....

....

4. Let's explore how God has promised this throughout history. Discuss the following verses.

- Leviticus 26:11-13

....

....

....
....
....
....

- Ezekiel 37:27-28

....
....
....
....
....
....

- 2 Corinthians 6:16

....
....
....
....
....
....

- John 14:2-3

....
....
....
....

....

....

DAY 3

1. After you spend time praying, read Revelation 21:5-8. Who is speaking?

....

....

....

....

....

....

2. What is His first great claim in verse 5?

....

....

....

....

....

....

3. Why does God want John to write these words, according to verse 5?

....

....

....

....

....

....

- Look at Revelation 19:11. What is the name of the rider on the white horse?

....

....

....

- What is your personal experience with these characteristics that define God and Jesus? How have you found Him to be faithful, trustworthy and true in your own life?

....

....

....

....

....

....

4. What does God say about Himself in verses 6-7?

....

....

....

....

....

....

5. Who is the recipient of God's love? Who is not?

....

....

....

....

....

....

6. Do you identify more as a conqueror or as cowardly and faithless? Bring this before God. If you are resting secure in your victory in Jesus, praise the Lord for that. If you are uncertain or doubting, talk to Him about it. Pray as the father of the demon-possessed boy did: 'I believe; help my unbelief!' (Mark 9:24). Whether you realize it or not, if you place your trust in Jesus, you are a conqueror and child of God. Even if your faith feels puny, your heritage is that you will dwell with the Lord forever.

....

....

....

DAY 4

1. The verses we read today will paint an intriguing picture in our minds. Do not get caught up in the unknowns of what some of the imagery means, but instead bask in the overall picture of the splendor found within the New Jerusalem. Start by reading Revelation 21:9-22.

2. In this vision, an angel whisks John away 'in the Spirit' and we see an unfolding of what we first read about in 21:2. What does John see in verses 10-14? What metaphor is used for its beauty?

....

....

....

....

....

....

3. Read verses 15-21. What do you gather about the New Jerusalem from these verses?

....

....

....

....

....

....

*Note that 12,000 stadia is roughly 1,380 miles. This is approximately the distance from Chicago, IL to Miami, FL. Point being—this city is *enormous!*

4. What does verse 22 tell us about the temple? Remember, in the ancient world, *every* city had some sort of temple.

....

....

....

....

....

....

5. By the same token, what do verses 23-24 tell us about the source of light in this city? Who gives the light and who is the lamp that shines forth the light? See also 22:5.

....

....

....

....

....

....

6. According to verses 24-27 who will walk in the light? What will they bring? Remember verse 21:8, which tells us who will *not* walk in the light.

....

....

....

....

....

....

We will walk in the pure light of God's presence when our eternal hope is finally realized in the new heavens and the new earth! That is a hope worth rejoicing in.

DAY 5

1. Let's read the final five verses of this study: Revelation 22:1-5. What does the angel show John next inside the city of the New Jerusalem? Describe the scene from verses 1-2 in your own words.

....

....

....

....

....

....

2. What does John say about:

- the river?

    ....

    ....

    ....

- the throne?

    ....

    ....

    ....

- the tree of life?

    ....

    ....

    ....

3. We see the throne of God and of the Lamb as the source of the living water. Read Revelation 7:17. What does this verse say about the Lamb?

....

....

....

....

....

....

• How does it relate to Revelation 22:1?

....

....

....

....

....

....

• Read Zechariah 13:7-9 and Matthew 26:30-32. What had to first
  happen to the Shepherd before He could become the exalted
  Lamb that we see in Revelation?

....

....

....

....

....

....

• Can you think of other places in Scripture that speak of living
  water?

....

....

....

....

....

....

- Has your spiritual thirst been quenched by the living water that Jesus offers?

....

....

....

....

....

....

4. According to 22:3, what will be absent from the city of God? In addition to God and the Lamb, who else will be present?

....

....

....

....

....

....

- What will they be doing? (Read another translation such as the NIV and read Revelation 7:15)

....

....

....

....

....

....

- What will they see, as verse 4 tells us?

....

....

....

....

....

....

- What do you think it means when John writes, 'his name will be on their foreheads'?

....

....

....

....

....

....

5. In verse 5 John again talks about the source of light, but in this verse it is mentioned as a gift to the Lord's servants. He then says that they will reign. How long will this kingdom in which they reign last?

....

....

....

....

....

....

I would like to close out this chapter with an excerpt from the book *Heaven* by Randy Alcorn. I do not think I could conclude this section with words better than his, so why try to reinvent the wheel?! Alcorn writes,[9]

> We're told that we will serve God in Heaven (Rev. 7:15, 22:3). Service is active, not passive. It involves fulfilling responsibilities in which we expend energy. Work in Heaven won't be frustrating or fruitless; instead, it will involve lasting accomplishment, unhindered by decay and fatigue, enhanced by unlimited resources. We'll approach our work with the enthusiasm we bring to our favorite sport or hobby.
>
> In Heaven, we'll reign with Christ, exercise leadership and authority, and make important decisions. This implies we'll be given specific responsibilities by our leaders and we'll delegate specific responsibilities to those under our leadership (Luke 19:17-19). We'll set goals, devise plans, and share ideas. Our best work days on the present Earth—those days when everything turns out better than we planned, when we get everything done on time, and when everyone on the team pulls together and enjoys each other—are just a small foretaste of the joy our work will bring us on the New Earth.

Though we're currently gazing at that dim reflection in the mirror, our work, free from the curse of sin, will one day be pure and fruitful and satisfying in every way. We will worship the Lord in joy and serve him in gladness. We will dwell with him *forever and ever!* Please

---

9   Alcorn, Randy. *Heaven*, p. 412.

pray through Psalm 100 with me as we end our study of the Good
Shepherd.

> Make a joyful noise to the Lord, all the earth!
> Serve the Lord with gladness!
> Come into his presence with singing!

> Know that the Lord, he is God!
> It is he who made us, and we are his;
> we are his people, and the sheep of his pasture.

> Enter his gates with thanksgiving,
> and his courts with praise!
> Give thanks to him; bless his name!

> For the Lord is good;
> his steadfast love endures forever,
> and his faithfulness to all generations.

We are the sheep of His pasture, and He is the Great Shepherd who
guides us, provides for us, protects us and loves us. His steadfast love
endures forever. I pray that this truth has become strikingly clear as
we've studied God as our Shepherd in both the Old Testament and
the New. Friends, do you see how intimately and lovingly the Lord
knows you? And through His Word, He is made *known* to you! Praise
Him for this glorious gift!

Surely goodness and mercy shall follow me all the days of my life, and I shall dwell in the house of the Lord forever.

PSALM 23:6

APPENDIX

Tracing a Biblical Theme[1]

Biblical Theme:

The Lord as our Shepherd

Creation:

Genesis 1:24-25—God creates land animals—livestock

Genesis 1:26—God creates man and gives him dominion over all

Genesis 2:19-20—God creates animals and birds and allows man to name them

The Fall:

Genesis 3:14—serpent is cursed 'above all livestock'—the curse falls on all of creation

Genesis 3:21—God clothes Adam and Eve with animal skins—death of animals

Pentateuch (Genesis–Deuteronomy):

Genesis 29:3, 46:32—duties of shepherds

Genesis 46:34, 47:3—protection/distinct people in Egypt because they are shepherds

Genesis 48:15—Jacob is the first to claim God as his shepherd

---

1 *Biblical Theology Workshop for Women with Nancy Guthrie.* Sept. 20-21, 2019 at Sojourn Church East, Louisville KY.

Genesis 49:24—'Mighty One of Jacob (from there is the Shepherd, the Stone of Israel)'

Exodus 2:17—Moses saves the priest of Midian's daughters from shepherds. Marries daughter Zipporah; ironically enough he will be one to shepherd Israel

Numbers 14:33—'Your children shall be shepherds in the wilderness forty years'

Numbers 27:17—God has Moses appoint Joshua to lead so they will not be 'as sheep that have no shepherd'

OT History (Judges–Esther):

1 Samuel 17:40—we meet David the shepherd about to conquer Goliath

2 Samuel 5:2, 1 Chronicles 11:1-3—David anointed as king; appointed as shepherd over God's people

2 Samuel 7:7, 1 Chronicles 17:6—judges had been commanded to shepherd God's people

1 Kings 22:17, 2 Chronicles 18:16—Prophet Micaiah sees Israel scattered as sheep without a shepherd

OT Wisdom (Job–Song of Songs):

Psalm 23, 28:9—be their shepherd and carry them forever

Psalm 49:14—death will be a shepherd to the foolish, pompous

Psalm 78:70-72—David to shepherd Israel

Psalm 80:1—'Shepherd of Israel, you who lead Joseph like a flock. You who are enthroned upon the cherubim, shine forth.' — shepherd king

Ecclesiastes 12:11—words given by one Shepherd

Song of Solomon 1:8—words in a love song

OT Prophets (Isaiah–Malachi):

Isaiah 13:14, 20—judgment against Babylon

Isaiah 40:11—'He will tend his flock like a shepherd; he will gather the lambs…'

Isaiah 44:28—Cyrus to accomplish his purposes in ending the seventy-year exile

Isaiah 63:11—God led His people with shepherds

Jeremiah 3:15—'I will give you shepherds after my own heart'

Jeremiah 6:3, 10:21, 12:10, 22:22, 23:1-2, 25:34-36, 50:6—shepherds apart from the Lord have led people astray

Jeremiah 17:16—'I have not run away from being your shepherd'

Jeremiah 23:4—'I will set shepherds over them who will care for them…'

Jeremiah 31:10—'he who scattered Israel will gather him'

Jeremiah 33:12—there will again be shepherds resting their flocks (restoration)

Jeremiah 43:12—cleansing as a shepherd does

Ezekiel 34:1-10—edict against shepherds

Ezekiel 34:11-24—the Lord as Shepherd

Amos 3:12—'As the shepherd rescues…so shall the people of Israel…be rescued'

Micah 5:4-5—'he shall stand and shepherd his flock in the strength of the Lord…'

Micah 7:14—'Shepherd your people with your staff…'

Zephaniah 2:6—restoration: shall be pastures, with meadows for shepherds

Zechariah 10:2-3, 11:3-5, 11:17—bad shepherds

Zechariah 13:7—strike the shepherd and the sheep will be scattered (Messianic)

The Gospels:

Matthew 2:6—wise men report king of the Jews to Herod; chief priests and scribes reveal Scripture prophecy: 'And you, O Bethlehem…from you shall come a ruler who will shepherd my people Israel.'

Matthew 9:36, Mark 6:34—Jesus has compassion for the crowds… like sheep without a shepherd

Matthew 25:32—final judgment—separate people as a shepherd separates sheep/goats

Matthew 26:31, Mark 14:27—Jesus predicting death—fulfills Zech. 13:7

Luke 2:8-20—Jesus' birth. Shepherds play huge role in announcing His birth

John 10:2—'he who enters by the door is the shepherd'

John 10:11—'I am the good shepherd…lays down his life for the sheep'

John 10:12—hired hand is not the shepherd…leaves the sheep and flees

John 10:14—'I am the good shepherd. I know my own and my own know me'

John 10:16—'I have other sheep that are not of this fold…there will be one flock, one shepherd'

Cross/Resurrection/Ascension/Pentecost (Gospels and Acts):

Matthew 26:31, Mark 14:27—strike the shepherd

John 10:11—lays down His life for the sheep

Epistles:

Hebrews 13:20-21—the great shepherd of the sheep, by the blood of the eternal covenant, equip you with everything good that you may do His will…

Ephesians 4:11—different jobs in the body of Christ—one is to shepherd

1 Peter 2:25—now returned to the Shepherd and Overseer of your soul

1 Peter 5:2—exhortation to shepherd the flock

Consummation:

1 Peter 5:4—'And when the chief Shepherd appears, you will receive the unfading crown of glory'

Revelation 7:17—'For the Lamb in the midst of the throne will be their shepherd, and he will guide them to springs of living water…'

RESOURCES

Alcorn, Randy. *Heaven*. Carol Stream: Tyndale House Publishers, Inc, 2004.

Alexander, Ralph H. *Ezekiel*. The Expositor's Bible Commentary. Vol. 6. Grand Rapids: Zondervan, 1986.

Bullock, C. Hassell. *Psalms Volume 1: Psalms 1-72*. Teach the Text Commentary Series. Grand Rapids: Baker Publishing Group, 2015.

Carter, Matt and Wredberg, Josh. *Christ-Centered Exposition: Exalting Jesus in John*. Nashville: B&H Publishing Group, 2017.

Clarke, Adam. 'Commentary on Psalms 30:4.' *The Adam Clarke Commentary*. 1832. https://www.studylight.org/commentaries/acc/psalms-30.html

Community Bible Study. *Isaiah*. Vol. 2 Lessons 16-30. Colorado Springs: Community Bible Study, 2015.

Community Bible Study. *1 and 2 Corinthians*. Vol. 2 Lessons 16-30. Colorado Springs: Community Bible Study, 2014.

Davis, Andrew M. *Christ-Centered Exposition: Exalting Jesus in Isaiah*. Nashville: B&H Publishing Group, 2017.

Dever, Mark. *The Message of the Old Testament*. Wheaton: Crossway Books, 2006.

Duguid, Iain M. *Ezekiel*. The NIV Application Commentary. Grand Rapids: Zondervan, 1999.

Duguid, Iain M. Hamilton Jr., James M., Skar, J *ESV Expository Commentary*. Vol 4: John-Acts. Wheaton: Crossway, 2019.

The Expositor's Bible Commentary. 1 Peter and Romans. Text Courtesy of BibleSupport.com on Biblehub.com. https://biblehub.com/commentaries/expositors

Goodrick, Edward W., *The Strongest NIV Exhaustive Concordance* (Grand Rapids, MI: Zondervan, 2004).

Grudem, Wayne. *Systematic Theology*. Grand Rapids: Zondervan, 1994.

Guthrie, Nancy. 'Biblical Theology Workshop for Women.' Sept. 20-21, 2019 at Sojourn Church East, Louisville KY. https://www.nancyguthrie.com/biblical-theology-workshop

Guzik, David. *The Enduring Word Bible Commentary*. https://enduringword.com/

Hughes, R. Kent. *John: That You May Believe*. Wheaton: Crossway, 2014.

'Introduction to Ezekiel.' *esv.org*. 2001-2020 Crossway. https://www.esv.org/resources/esv-global-study-bible/introduction-to-ezekiel/

'Introduction to Revelation.' *esv.org*. 2001-2020 Crossway. https://www.esv.org/resources/esv-global-study-bible/introduction-to-revelation/

Jamison, Kevin. 'Faith Alone.' Sermon preached at Sojourn Church East on Nov. 5, 2017.

Keller, W. Phillip. *A Shepherd Looks at Psalm 23*. Grand Rapids: Zondervan, 1970.

Lewis, C.S. *Mere Christianity*. New York: Macmillan Publishing Company, 1943.

Mounce, William D. *Mounce's Complete Expository Dictionary of Old & New Testament Words*. Grand Rapids: Zondervan, 2006.

RESOURCES

Nielson, Kathleen Buswell. *John: That You May Believe.* Living Word Bible Studies. Phillipsburg: P&R Publishing, 2010.

Pennington, Jonathan. 'Hoping Through Suffering.' Sermon preached for Sojourn Church East on April 4, 2020. https://www.youtube.com/watch?v=2NaTwQj4A6A

Piper, John. 'Faith and the Imputation of Righteousness.' Sermon preached on Oct. 17, 1999. Desiringgod.org/scripture/romans/4/messages

Piper, John. 'The Inexplicable Life: Humility, Hope & Love in Suffering.' The Gospel Coalition Women's Conference, Indianapolis. June 18, 2016. Desiringgod.org/messages/the-inexplicable-life

Piper, John. 'Why We Can Rejoice in Suffering.' Sermon preached on Oct. 23, 1994. Desiringgod.org

Reeves, Michael. *Did You Know That Charles Spurgeon Struggled With Depression?* Feb. 24, 2018. *https://www.crossway.org/articles/did-you-know-that-charles-spurgeon-struggled-with-depression/*

Rothschild, Jennifer. *Psalm 23: The Shepherd with Me.* Nashville: LifeWay Press, 2018.

Ryken, Leland, Wilhoit, James C, Longman III, Tremper General Editors. *Dictionary of Biblical Imagery.* Downers Grove: InterVarsity Press, 1998.

Schreiner, Thomas R. *Romans.* Baker Books: Grand Rapids, 1998.

Spurgeon, Charles H. *Lectures to My Students, Addresses Delivered to the Students of the Pastors' College, Metropolitan Tabernacle.* New York: Robert Carter and Brothers, 1889, vol. 1.

Taylor, John B. *Ezekiel: An Introduction and Commentary.* Tyndale Old Testament Commentaries. Downers Grove: InterVarsity Press, 2016.

Wiersbe, Warren W. *Be Alive: Get to Know the Living Savior.* NT Commentary John 1-12. Colorado Springs: David C Cook, 1986.

Wiersbe, Warren W. *Be Comforted: Feeling Secure in the Arms of God.* OT Commentary Isaiah. Colorado Springs: David C Cook, 1992.

Wiersbe, Warren W. *Be Hopeful: How to Make the Best of Times out of Your Worst of Times.* NT Commentary 1 Peter. Colorado Springs: David C Cook, 1982.

Wiersbe, Warren W. *Be Transformed: Christ's Triumph Means Your Transformation.* NT Commentary John 13-21. Colorado Springs: David C Cook, 1986.

Wiersbe, Warren W. *Be Worshipful: Glorifying God for Who He Is.* OT Commentary Psalms 1-89. Colorado Springs: David C Cook, 2004.

Wright, N.T. *1 & 2 Peter and Jude: 9 Studies for Individuals and Groups.* N.T. Wright for Everyone Bible Study Guides. Downers Grove: InterVarsity Press, 2012.

Youngblood, Ronald F., General Editor. *Nelson's New Illustrated Bible Dictionary.* Nashville: Thomas Nelson Publishers, 1995.

Christian Focus Publications

Our mission statement —

STAYING FAITHFUL

In dependence upon God we seek to impact the world through literature faithful to His infallible Word, the Bible. Our aim is to ensure that the Lord Jesus Christ is presented as the only hope to obtain forgiveness of sin, live a useful life and look forward to heaven with Him.

Our books are published in four imprints:

CHRISTIAN
FOCUS

Popular works including biographies, commentaries, basic doctrine and Christian living.

CHRISTIAN
HERITAGE

Books representing some of the best material from the rich heritage of the church.

MENTOR

Books written at a level suitable for Bible College and seminary students, pastors, and other serious readers. The imprint includes commentaries, doctrinal studies, examination of current issues and church history.

CF4•K

Children's books for quality Bible teaching and for all age groups: Sunday school curriculum, puzzle and activity books; personal and family devotional titles, biographies and inspirational stories — because you are never too young to know Jesus!

Christian Focus Publications Ltd,
Geanies House, Fearn, Ross-shire,
IV20 1TW, Scotland, United Kingdom.
www.christianfocus.com